50
Graphic Organizers
for Reading, Writing & More

Reproducible Templates, Student Samples, and
Easy Strategies to Support Every Learner

Linda Irwin-DeVitis

Karen Bromley

Marcia Modlo

SCHOLASTIC
PROFESSIONAL BOOKS

NEW YORK • TORONTO • LONDON • AUCKLAND • SYDNEY
MEXICO CITY • NEW DELHI • HONG KONG

Dedication

*This book is dedicated to all the students and teachers with whom
we have worked. We have learned much from them
and their willingness to try new ideas.
Their creativity, patience, and persistence are our inspiration.*

Acknowledgments

We would like to thank our graduate students, and the teachers and their students who have contributed their ideas, samples of their work, and their enthusiasm for this project. In particular, our appreciation to those who contributed sample graphic organizers: Laura Brigham, Kathy Buckner, Tracy D'Arpino, Rebecca J. Beers, Janelle L. Billings, Elsa Bingel, Sheri Brewer, Lynda DeLuca, Lynne Eckert, Angela Elsbree, Sarah Evans, Deborah Griesinger, Nancy B. Hargrave, Linda Hoffman, Linda Hopkins, Luci Huizinga, Sloan M. Johnson, Gregory Lehr, Michelle Keough Lehr, Diane Leskow, Pat Lynch, Lizanne McTigue, Rose Rotzler, Colleen Schultz, Carrie Van Vorce, and Karen Wassell. We would also like to thank our editors at Scholastic Professional Books, Virginia Dooley and Terry Cooper, for their support for the book.

ISBN 0-590-00484-0
Cover design by Drew Hires
Interior design by Solutions by Design, Inc.
Interior illustrations by Teresa Anderko

Table of Contents

PART I

Introduction

Many readers of our first book, *Graphic Organizers: Visual Strategies for Active Learning, K-8,* have asked us for additional examples of graphic organizers, strategies for using them, and full-size templates to support classroom use. This book is our answer to those requests. We hope the specific procedures, variations, and examples of organizers in the book will encourage and support the use of graphic organizers as a valuable tool for students and teachers in their thinking and learning.

What is a graphic organizer?

A graphic organizer is a visual representation of knowledge that structures information by arranging important aspects of a concept or topic into a pattern using labels. You may see and hear a variety of other names for the graphic organizer, including semantic map, visual organizer, structured overview, story web, or mind map.

Graphic organizers are wonderful strategies to get students actively involved in their learning. Because graphic organizers include both words and visual images, they are effective with a wide variety of learners, including ESL, gifted, and special-needs students. Graphic organizers present information in concise ways that highlight the organization and relationships of concepts. They can be used with any subject matter at any level. Daniel H. Robinson (1998) reviewed the research on graphic organizers and suggests that teachers and researchers use only those organizers that are easily created by amateurs. He also suggests the use of a variety of types of organizers chosen for their appropriateness for the content. They are effective tools in planning, instruction, and assessment.

Reasons for using graphic organizers

- ⊙ Graphic organizers help you and your students focus on what is important because they highlight key concepts and vocabulary, and the relationships among them, thus providing the tools for critical and creative thinking (Bromley, Irwin-DeVitis, and Modlo, 1995).

- ⊙ The human mind organizes and stores information in a series of networks (Ausubel, 1968). Graphic organizers are visual depictions that resemble networks and allow students to add or modify their background knowledge by seeing the connections and contradictions between existing knowledge (schemas) and new information. This is consistent with Piaget's (1974) notions of assimilation and accommodation in learning.

- ⊙ Graphic organizers serve as mental tools, Vygotsky's (1962) semiotic mediators, to help the learner remember. The information in a graphic organizer is visual as well as verbal; highlights the relationships between ideas; and focuses on the most important information. Thus, the learner is better able to understand and retain the material.

- ⊙ Constructing or evaluating graphic organizers requires the student to be actively involved with the information. Both when working independently and working with others, the dialogue and decision making required to construct graphic organizers promote interaction with the material (Novak and Gowin, 1984).

- The negotiation and coconstruction of meaning that is integral to the creation of graphic organizers allows students to build on one another's knowledge (Bromley, et al., 1995).

- Graphic organizers are effective with diverse students in a variety of settings. For example, Cassidy (1991) found graphic organizers improved the learning of gifted students; both Lehman (1992) and Sorenson (1991) found them effective for students with special needs. Graphic organizers can be particularly beneficial for students who have difficulty with composing. They provide an optional way of depicting knowledge and understanding.

- Individual students who use graphic organizers in the classroom develop their ability to use them independently as study tools for note taking, planning, presentation, and review (Dunston, 1992).

- Graphic organizers are used more and more often in business, industry, and print and electronic media. The ability to interpret, critique, and create these organizers is a part of visual literacy now considered basic to education (Cairney, 1997; Moline, 1995). Currently, viewing is considered the fifth language art, and teachers are urged to develop it with their students at all grade levels.

- Graphic organizers are viable alternatives to more traditional assessments. Teachers have successfully used graphic organizers to monitor learning by having students construct them before a topic or unit of study, and then adding or modifying the organizer as they gain added knowledge through reading and research (Irwin-DeVitis and Pease, 1995). Using organizers for the final assessment focuses both students and teachers on the key concepts and the relationships among these concepts. Remember, when using graphic oranizers for assessment, students should have the option to explain their organizer and defend their reasoning. This combination of oral or written explanation and the visual depiction of the knowledge provides powerful insights into students' learning and provides valuable feedback on instructional design and implementation.

- More and more often, textbooks are using graphic organizers. Students and teachers need to be able to evaluate the organizers and use them as models and learning aids (Robinson, 1998). In addition, new assessments for literacy and the content areas from commercial publishers and state departments are including graphic organizers.

Types of graphic organizers

While there are many variations and possible combinations of organizers, most of them fall into four basic categories.

Conceptual: These types of graphic organizer include a main concept or central idea with supporting facts, evidence, or characteristics. Some common examples are webs, Venn diagrams, and central question organizers. The Big Question (p. 18), Mind Map (p. 54), and Getting into Character (p. 42) organizers fall into this category.

Hierarchical: These organizers begin with a topic or concept and then include a number of ranks or levels below the topic. The key characteristic of the pattern is that there are distinct levels that proceed from top to bottom or bottom to top. The position on the organizer denotes the level of the label within the organization. We have included the Hierarchical Organizer (p. 44) and Main Idea Pyramid templates (p. 50) as examples.

Cyclical: The cyclical organizer depicts a series of events without beginning or end. The formation is circular and continuous. An example is the Circle Organizer (p. 26).

Sequential: Sequential organizers arrange events in chronological order. This type of organizer is helpful when events have a specific beginning and end. It is also appropriate for cause-and-effect, process-and-product and problem-solution text. The pattern is linear, as in a timeline. Examples are the Plot Diagram (p. 66) and the Multiple Timeline (p. 60).

Of course, the number of variations and combinations of these basic types are only limited by the ingenuity of the students and teachers who create them.

Deciding what type of organizer to use

The content and organization of material usually determines the type of organizer to be created. Another factor is the learning or cognitive style of the person creating the organizer. Individuals will often have a preference for one type of graphic organizer or another. The nonlinear and open-ended quality of the conceptual organizer is often appealing to more holistic, creative thinkers. The super-ordinate/subordinate structure of the hierarchical organizer and chronological structure of the sequential organizer may appeal more to those who think linearly and logically. More importantly, having experiences with a variety of organizers allows you and your students to pick and choose the type most appropriate for the subject and purpose.

Constructing your own graphic organizer

We've provided you with 50 ready-to-use templates in this book. But you may want to develop your own graphic organizers. Here's how to do it.

1. Identify the main ideas. This can be done through brainstorming a list or through examination of the text. Sometimes the key concepts are highlighted or appear as major headings. When brainstorming with students, be sure to accept all ideas.

2. Cluster or group words and ideas that are related.

3. Determine the relationships between and among the main ideas (cause and effect, sequential or chronological, main idea and supporting details, hierarchical, comparative, etc.) and choose the type of organizer most appropriate for the material and the purpose.

4. Arrange ideas and draw the connecting lines between and among them. At this point, you may eliminate items from the brainstorming list that are not appropriate. You can also label the lines with words that describe the relationship or link the information.

5. Recognize that often there are many ways to represent the information and to connect the concepts.

6. Use icons and pictures as well as words in your organizer.

7. Use a variety of colors to represent aspects of the organizer or the contributions of different individuals or groups.

8. Give students partially constructed graphic organizers to complete before you expect them to create organizers independently. Your goal should be to move from direct instruction and modeling to student independence in the creation of organizers.

Graphic organizers can be constructed:

- on blackboards
- for use with overhead projectors
- on flannel boards
- on chart paper
- on standard-size paper that can be copied for each student

Various tools can be used to construct the organizers:

- Colored markers or pencils can be used to highlight different topics or to identify individual contributions to a group organizer.
- Computer software (see the list on page 10) allows students of all ages to employ graphics and produce professional-looking flow charts and organizers.

Inspiration 5.0. (1997). Inspiration Software, Inc., 7412 SE Beaverton Hillsdale Highway, Suite 102, Beaverton, OR 97225

Kid Pix. Broderbund Software, Inc., 17 Paul Drive, San Rafael, CA 94903-2101.

The Learning Tool. Intellimation, P.O. Box 1911, Santa Barbara, CA 93116-1911

Mighty Draw. Macintosh and Windows versions. Abracadata, Ltd., Eugene, OR.

Mind Map. William K. Bradford Publishing Co., 16 Craig Road, Acton, MA 01720.

Semantic Mapper. Teacher Support Software, 1035 N. X. 57th Street, Gainesville, FL 32605-4486.

SemNet. Available from Kathleen M. Fisher, Center for Research in Mathematics and Science Education, 6475 Alvarado Road, Suite 206, San Diego State University, San Diego, CA 92103.

STELLA® software. High Performance Systems, 45 Lyme Road, Hanover, NH 03755.

VisiMap and *VisiMapLite.* Buzan Centre of Toronto, 30 Elm Avenue, Suite 206, Toronto, Ontario M4W INS, CANADA.

Grouping students when using graphic organizers

Students may create organizers individually, in groups, or in whole-class settings. When students are learning about graphic organizers, they will do best when you provide direct instruction and model the process for them. As they become more knowledgeable, students will be able to create organizers in collaborative groups and independently. It is best to begin with some of the simpler organizers. Conceptual and sequential organizers are often the easiest for students to understand and use. Of course, you will want to demonstrate graphic organizers on material that is familiar to you and your students.

What social skills are necessary?

The social skills needed for group work are those that are frequently identified and taught in cooperative-learning approaches. Listening, speaking, questioning, turn-taking, providing positive and constructive responses, and respecting others' opinions are important for any collaboration to be effective. Negotiation, consensus building, and teamwork are critical skills for individuals and groups in school and in life. These skills are discussed and more detailed examples of the thinking and sharing processes involved in students' meaning construction are included in *Graphic Organizers: Visual Strategies for Active Learning* (1995). A checklist to help students monitor and assess their group work is helpful. The checklist on the next page will help you and your students discuss and evaluate their group and individual social skills as they create organizers collaboratively.

Collaborative Group Checklist

Circle the number which applies.

	Disagree				Agree
I/we had a clear goal(s).	1	2	3	4	5
I/we made progress toward the goals.	1	2	3	4	5
I/we accomplished the goals.	1	2	3	4	5
I/we stayed on task.	1	2	3	4	5
I/we took turns talking.	1	2	3	4	5
I/we listened to others.	1	2	3	4	5
I/everyone contributed.	1	2	3	4	5
I/we respected others' opinions.	1	2	3	4	5
I/we asked questions.	1	2	3	4	5
I/we helped each other.	1	2	3	4	5
I/we negotiated solutions.	1	2	3	4	5
I/we gave positive feedback.	1	2	3	4	5

Some important reminders:

⊙ Discussion of the concepts and relationships is a key aspect of learning because it allows students to build on and clarify one another's knowledge. Without discussion, graphic organizers are not as effective in supporting learning.

⊙ Learning is enhanced when students create their own graphic organizers. Active engagement with the material is necessary to create an organizer since processing information is a key factor in learning.

⊙ Information can be represented in many ways. There is no one right way to represent material visually.

⊙ Some students are more visual than others in their learning. For these students, graphic organizers are particularly helpful.

⊙ Graphic organizers are appropriate for diverse learners because using key vocabulary and pictures or icons makes learning language easier. Graphic organizers can be particularly helpful to ESL students as they highlight the key ideas, important vocabulary, and their connections with a minimal amount of language.

Using the templates and strategies in this book

While we have provided a number of ideas and strategies, we hope that this book will be a useful guide and resource to stimulate your own ideas and variations. In many cases, the templates and ideas will transfer directly to the text you wish to use. At other times, you will need to modify the templates to meet your needs. For instance, the Hierarchical Organizer (p. 44) has three levels. You may want to delete the third level or add a fourth. You may need more or fewer boxes in a level. The decision to modify the template before you give it to students or to work with them to modify the template will depend upon their developmental level and their experience with graphic organizers. Certainly, the modification of a template to fit specific text is an opportunity for critical thinking. It is important that students understand that the template should be constructed or adapted to match the information, not vice versa.

As you work with students using graphic organizers, you will see a number of positive developments:

- ⊙ improved social skills

- ⊙ an emphasis on process-oriented, strategic learning

- ⊙ improved questioning ability

- ⊙ reflective and negotiated decision making

- ⊙ critical thinking and higher-level reasoning

- ⊙ more positive attitudes toward learning

- ⊙ increased understanding of the different ways of viewing information that may be influenced by personality, culture and life experiences

- ⊙ better understanding and retention of content

For some students, graphic organizers will become a preferred learning and study strategy. For others, the ability to create and use graphic organizers will be a valuable addition to their repertoire of study skills. We believe that graphic organizers are valuable strategies for effective learning that will help teachers and students in increasingly diverse classrooms improve learning, achieve high standards, and promote critical thinking.

COMMON QUESTIONS AND ANSWERS

1. **How do I know when to use a template and when to have students create a graphic organizer on their own?**

A template provides an organizational framework for students who are new to graphic organizers or those unfamiliar with the structure of a particular text. Use templates with students only as long as they need this support. When students have the confidence to create graphic organizers on their own, encourage them to construct the organizers independent of a predetermined structure that you have identified. Creating one's own organizer requires processing information differently and perhaps more deeply than if you were supplying information to complete a partially constructed organizer. Research evidence points to improved learning and memory for ideas and information when students create their own organizers.

2. What are some ways to assess with graphic organizers?

It is best to use graphic organizers to assess knowledge only when you and your students have used them extensively so students are comfortable with them. Asking students to create graphic organizers is a realistic alternative to a written essay question or brainstorming as part of prewriting. For students who have disabilities in writing or are slow writers, this method allows them to demonstrate their understandings of content by representing ideas and information and the relationships among them. Of course, a conference with the student is an integral part of this process so he or she can explain the organizer.

3. Is it better to choose one particular type of graphic organizer to use with my class at first?

Yes, you may want to begin with one type until your students are familiar with it before you move on to exploring other types with them. But remember that the content of text or a presentation determines the type of organizer. For example, not all content can be best represented with a hierarchical organizer. Be sure to model the creation of each type of organizer with appropriate material several times. Also, creating organizers on chart paper or the computer and posting them on bulletin boards helps familiarize students with their form. Many teachers tell us that having their students work in small groups and pairs to create organizers together is also helpful before they create them independently.

4. I don't want to bore my students, so how often is too often to use graphic organizers in my class?

Like anything else, use common sense and be sensitive to the attitudes and feelings of your students about overuse of a strategy. Their behavior and affect will be key. Be sure to coordinate your use of graphic organizers with other teachers so you can see what graphic organizers they're using, in which subjects, and how often. Also, don't forget that the best way to avoid burnout with a particular strategy is to be flexible. Vary the format by using small groups and pairs; allowing students to use chart paper, colored paper, or the computer to create organizers; and giving them choices in colored pens, markers, or pencils. Of course, using a computer program (see Chapter 1 or Professional References) to create organizers or put them in final publishable form for a class presentation is highly motivational for many students.

5. Are graphic organizers useful with diverse learners?

Yes, graphic organizers are particularly helpful for ESL students, students with learning disabilities and special needs, and gifted students. Graphic organizers highlight "key" vocabulary and can include pictures, both of which give these students a concise visual that helps them learn and remember information and understand relationships. Students for whom language is slow or delayed, and ESL learners need opportunities to use all their senses—visual, auditory, kinesthetic, and tactile as they discuss, problem-solve, research, and organize information together. Graphic organizers can help develop critical thinking for gifted students (Cassidy, 1989), the content area learning of secondary students with learning disabilities (Horton, 1990), and vocabulary for ESL students (Kaelin, 1991).

6. **In which subjects and at which grade level(s) do graphic organizers work best?**

Graphic organizers can be used across all grade levels and in all subject areas. Even the new assessments and latest standardized tests require students to summarize information as scaffolding for writing. Elementary and middle school teachers are doing exciting work with graphic organizers in their planning, teaching, and assessment. In our work with teachers, we see graphic organizers used just as successfully by kindergarten teachers as by secondary gifted students and literacy specialists.

7. **How can I use graphic organizers in my teaching, instructional planning, and professional development?**

Graphic organizers are a versatile tool for planning since they allow you to brainstorm in a nonlinear way and add ideas as they come to you. Graphic organizers are the perfect format if you are collaboratively planning a unit with a colleague. They invite reflection, discussion, and revision. They also allow you to see new connections among ideas and content that you might not have seen if you were planning with an outline or in a more linear way. It's not uncommon to see graphic organizers used in staff-development workshops, by teachers and principals at faculty meetings, and by consultants, because they are a clear and concise way to communicate ideas and information. For example, a teacher and a reading specialist collaborated to make a presentation using graphic organizers to their colleagues on writing workshops. Much of what they conveyed with graphic organizers showed succinctly the essence of their implementation and management. We have also seen organizers used effectively to plan a meeting, profile a student, and guide a parent-teacher conference.

8. **Can parents work with their children to create graphic organizers?**

Yes, parental involvement in a student's school experience is always beneficial and working with a student to create graphic organizers is no different. Some parents may have expertise with flow charts or other types of graphic organizers in their workplace, but for those who don't, we suggest reading about the why's and how's of graphic organizers or attending a workshop on them. If a workshop is not available, you can give parents detailed written directions at a parent-teacher conference. When parents understand the *why* and the *how* of graphic organizers, they can work with their children using this strategy to aid learning.

9. What happens when a student volunteers an incorrect response to include in a graphic organizer?

It is important for you to consider the instructional purpose of the graphic organizer. If the purpose is to generate ideas via brainstorming, all responses given by students should be accepted. Later, as students read and research the topic, you and your students can clarify or correct misconceptions. Often, the student who volunteers an incorrect response is the one to suggest a clarification or modification based on his new learning.

If the purpose of the graphic organizer is to demonstrate learning, incorrect responses need to be addressed directly. Teachers and/or peers should note the incorrect response perhaps with a question or evidence to help the student see that her response is inappropriate so she can correct it.

10. What is the biggest problem or challenge I may experience with graphic organizers?

Most often, teachers say they lack enough time to create and use graphic organizers. But across curriculum areas, teachers who have had the opportunity to learn about graphic organizers and who use them regularly in their teaching are overwhelmingly enthusiastic about the potential of graphic organizers for enhancing understanding of content and learning in general. Graphic organizers take time to plan before a lesson, but they facilitate learning and retention.

11. Do graphic organizers really show teachers more about what students know than tests or essays do?

Graphic organizers can demonstrate a student's ability to identify key concepts and make connections among them. In a typical essay exam, written language ability, grammar, spelling, and style often are prerequisites for demonstrating knowledge. Writing essays in an organized and connected way is quite difficult for some students and can obscure their knowledge of content. Objective tests frequently measure information in isolation without furnishing a clear picture of the student's grasp of the "big picture." The creation of graphic organizers by students can show teachers how students view concepts and facts and their relationships. In an ideal situation, when a teacher uses a student's graphic organizer for assessment, the student provides the teacher with a verbal explanation as well. In this way, you may learn more about your student's knowledge than he is able to write. For these reasons, graphic organizers are an effective assessment option for students who lack writing fluency or are in emergent literacy stages.

12. What do you do when a student thinks his graphic representation is the best and only way to show a concept(s)?

You can help this student see that there are a variety of ways to represent ideas graphically. For example, at the conclusion of a unit, ask each student to create a graphic organizer to represent the unit's organizing concept.

Then ask volunteers to share their individually created graphic organizers with the class. Be sure to accept and praise the variety of organizers and information that is shared. You might also develop two or three organizers yourself to illustrate a concept, an idea, or information and share these with your students to demonstrate multiple ways of representing content. In these ways you can help such students broaden their thinking.

REFERENCES

Alvermann, D.E. (1991). "The discussion web: A graphic aid for learning across the curriculum." *The Reading Teacher*, (45)2, 92–99.

Ausubel, D.P. (1968). *Educational Psychology: A Cognitive View.* New York: Holt.

Bromley, K., Irwin-DeVitis, L. and Modlo, M. (1995). *Graphic Organizers: Visual Strategies for Active Learning.* New York: Scholastic Professional Books.

Cairney T. H. (1997). "New avenues to literacy." *Educational Leadership, 54,* 6. 76–77.

Cassidy, J.(1991)."Using graphic organizers to develop critical thinking." *Gifted Child Today,* 12 (6), 34–36.

Dunston, P. J. (1992). "A critique of graphic organizer research." *Reading Research and Instruction, 31* (2), 57–65.

Horton, V. (1990). The effectiveness of graphic organizers for three classifications of secondary students in content area classes. *Journal of Learning Disabilities,* 23 (1), 12–22.

Irwin-DeVitis, L. and Pease, D. (1995). "Using graphic organizers for learning and assessment in middle level classrooms." *Middle School Journal, 26* (5), 57–64.

Kaelin, A. (1991). *The Effects of Instruction Using a Mnemonic Graphic Organizer for Vocabulary Instruction Among Adult English as a Second Language Students.* Sacramento: California State University.

Lehman, H. (1992). "Graphic organizers benefit slow learners." *Clearinghouse, 66* (1), 53–55.

Moline, S. (1995). *I See What You Mean: Children at Work With Visual Information.* York, ME: Stenhouse.

Novak, J. D. and Gowin, D. B. (1984). *Learning How to Learn.* New York: Cambridge University Press.

Piaget, J. (1974). *The Thought and Language of the Child.* Translated by M. Gabain. New York: New American Library.

Robinson, D. H. (1998). "Graphic organizers as aids to text learning." *Reading Research and Instruction, 37,* (2), 85–105.

Sorenson, S. (1991). *Working with special students in English language arts.* TRIED, ED 336902, Bloomington, IN: ERIC Clearinghouse on Reading and Communication Skills.

Vygotsky, L. S. (1962). *Thought and Language.* Cambridge, MA: MIT Press.

PART II

Templates, Strategies, and Student Samples

In this section, we've included a variety of graphic organizers that can be used in many different curriculum areas. The first 34 are accompanied by step-by-step directions, student samples, and strategies for using them. The last ten are self-explanatory, so we included just the templates.

The Big Question Research Map

Description: Using a central, authentic question involves students in research and problem solving. Questions should be provocative and relevant to students' lives. Because this organizer requires students to plan their research and exploration of a topic, it promotes their ability to learn and think independently.

Procedures:

1. Use an authentic question, a question for which there is no easy, pre-existing answer or solution. It should be generated by a student or a group of students independently or in collaboration with the teacher.

2. Brainstorm the strategies, procedures, and resources needed to answer the question. (You can think of the big question as the *what*, and brainstorm the *who, when, where, why* and *how*.)

3. Record the information on the map.

4. Add, delete, or change the organizer as needed throughout the process of answering the big question.

Variations:

⊙ Provide the big question as a prereading activity. Students will predict the *who, when, where,* and *why* they expect to find in the reading.

⊙ Use this organizer to explore issues of classroom community by framing problems as questions and inviting students to brainstorm solutions.

⊙ Introduce a topic and have individuals or groups decide what the big question is, and then contrast the ways in which the different questions call for different approaches or resources.

⊙ Use the big question as a format for comparing how different authors answer the same question, for example, "What are nightmares?" Then students can look at how a variety of authors describe nightmares in their books.

This map was created with information from Beth and Pace Bartling at St. Joseph's Elementary School in Knoxville, Tennessee.

The Big Question

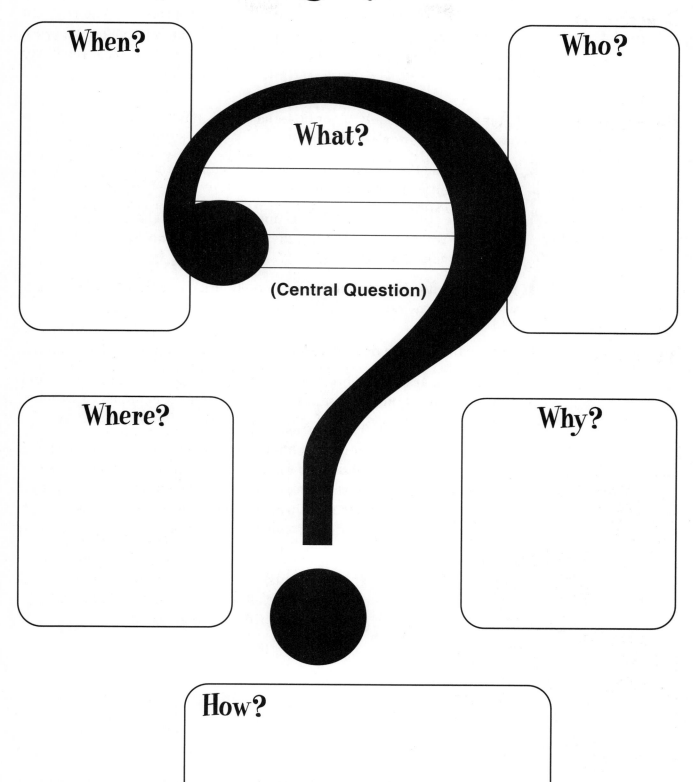

When?

Who?

What?

_____
_____
_____
_____

(Central Question)

Where?

Why?

How?

Bookmark Organizer

Description: This is a useful postreading activity. It is an authentic book report because it has a real purpose and audience. In addition, the bookmark can serve as a discussion guide during student-teacher or peer-reading conferences.

Procedures:

1. After students read a book or other selection, have them discuss the book with a peer or with you.

2. Following the discussion, have students complete the bookmark template following the directions.

3. Encourage students to use illustrations and icons in the sections, as well as words. You may want to have them use markers or crayons. Have them cut out the bookmarks.

4. Have students give their completed bookmarks to classmates they think would enjoy the book.

Variations:

⊙ Display bookmarks on bulletin boards, or on classroom or library walls.

⊙ Place bookmarks in the books so other readers can get a quick overview and evaluation from a classmate.

⊙ Vary the instructions for each block. Block 3 could ask students to rate the book's illustrations on a scale of one to four stars, with four being the best. Block 4 could ask students to rate the story itself on the same scale. Block 5 could ask students to describe the type of reader who would like the book.

⊙ Have students put other stories by the same author in Block 3; similar books in Block 4; and a favorite quote from the book in Block 5.

Book Mark Organizer

1. Write the title and author of the book.

1 TITLE: **Matilda**
AUTHOR: Roald Dahl

2. Tell what you liked or did not like about the story.

2 Matilda was smart. She didn't need to be "strong" to get by, she just used her nuggin.

3. Write the names or draw pictures of the main characters.

3 Matilda, her parents, the mean lady in the house, her teacher

4. Describe or draw the setting of the story.

4 the most exciting was the creepy house where the teacher lived

5. Tell about or draw an interesting event or character.

5 when Matilda made things happen...like when the teacher made her mad

Ryan Robinson - Sidney Middle School

Ryan Robinson created this organizer after his class read Matilda *by Roald Dahl. Ryan was a student at Sidney Middle School, Sidney, New York.*

50 Graphic Organizers for Reading, Writing, and More
Scholastic Professional Books, 1999

Bookmark Organizer

1. Write the title and author of the book.

1.

Title: _____

Author: _____

2. Tell what you liked or did not like about the story.

2.

3. Write the names or draw pictures of the main characters.

3.

4. Describe or draw the setting of the story.

4.

5. Tell about or draw an interesting event or character.

5.

Character Map

Description: This activity promotes critical and analytical thinking about literary characters and their key traits. Students must read closely and support their choices with evidence (literal or inferential) from the story. This may be done individually or in small groups.

Procedures:

1. Ask individuals or groups to select a character. Write the character's name in the central circle.

2. Have students identify the main traits of the character (or physical attributes) and put those in the diamonds directly connected to the character.

3. Annotate with quotes, actions, thoughts, or other evidence for each trait in the rectangles connected to that diamond (trait).

Variations:

⊙ The character map may be used with historical figures as well as with fictional characters.

⊙ Character maps may be used as prewriting organizers.

⊙ Character maps may be completed by different groups or individuals, and compared.

⊙ Students may keep character maps to document their independent reading. It may be interesting for them to look at the maps they have created over time to see what kinds of characters they enjoy in their reading.

⊙ After students have read one chapter in a book, have them use a character map to predict what a character will be like. Then have them complete a second map after completing the book. Use the maps as the basis for a discussion on character change (or on static and dynamic characters for more advanced students).

⊙ Put a historical event in the central circle and use the diamonds for major factors or causes and the rectangles for evidence supporting the identified causes.

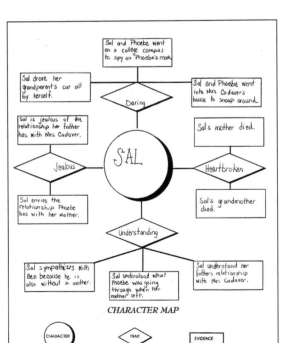

CHARACTER MAP

This map was created by Laura Brigham for the main character, Sal, in Walk Two Moons *by Sharon Creech.*

50 Graphic Organizers for Reading, Writing, and More
Scholastic Professional Books, 1999

Character Map

Character · Trait · Evidence

Character Relationships Map

Description: Students can understand the relationships among and between characters in a story with this map. By identifying and examining the feelings and emotions that accompany actions, students can better understand the complexities of individual characters and their interactions with one another.

Procedures:

1. Identify a main character from a book the class is reading or has just finished reading and put the character's name in the center circle on the template.

2. Put the names of secondary characters from the story in the other circles on the template.

3. Have students identify how the main character feels about each of the secondary characters.

4. Ask students to identify the actions or references from the text that support their ideas.

5. Record these ideas on the appropriate directional connector lines of the template.

6. Have students identify how the secondary characters feel about the main character and the actions or references involving the main character, and record these ideas on the appropriate lines.

7. Discuss with students how the interplay among characters' feelings and emotions can be both a cause and an effect leading to characters' actions or inertia.

Character Relationship Web

Variations:

⊙ Use this map to help students relate to characters from historical fiction, a genre they may have trouble understanding because the stories are set in another time period and characters often speak in unfamiliar language patterns.

⊙ To develop story involvement and understanding, have each student put his or her own name in the center circle, filling in the other circles with characters from the story. Have students write their feelings toward these characters.

A sixth grader in Michelle Keogh Lehr's class at Vestal Middle School created this map to show the relationships among characters in Molly's Pilgrim *by Barbara Cohen.*

50 Graphic Organizers for Reading, Writing, and More
Scholastic Professional Books, 1999

Name_____ Date _____

Character Relationships Web

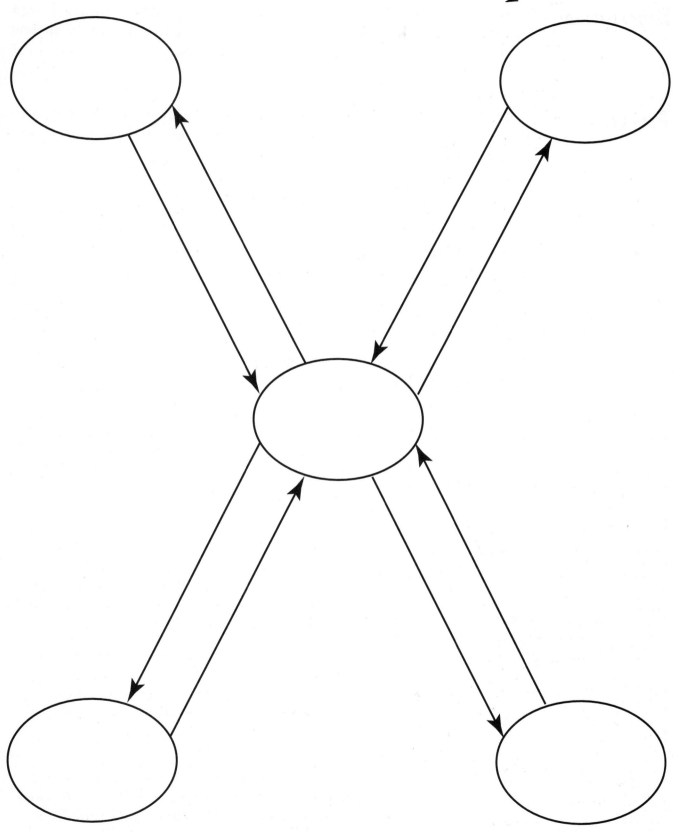

Circle Organizer

Description: This organizer shows the sequence of events in a process. In a sequence circle there is a consecutive flow of events with the last event cycling back to the first event. Sequence circles are only appropriate for processes that are continuous.

Procedures:

1. Discuss a cyclical process (rain cycle or animal life cycle, for example) with students. Encourage them to retell the sequence of events.

2. Add a label describing the process in the center of the template.

3. In clockwise order as the students relate them, write the events in the boxes provided. (Delete or add boxes as needed, depending on the process.)

4. Have students use the events to explain the steps in the process.

Variations:

⊙ Let the map become a blueprint for writing a story in which the events build on one another to a climax.

⊙ Encourage students to include drawings on their sequence circle to remind them of the steps of the process.

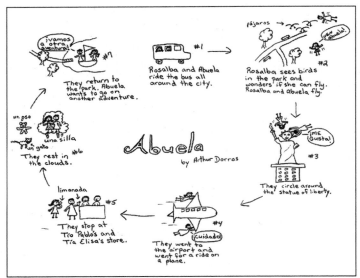

Sloan M. Johnson created this story circle for a small reading group based on Arthur Dorros's tale Abuela. *The circle includes a number of Spanish words with pictures and English explanations.*

Circle Organizer

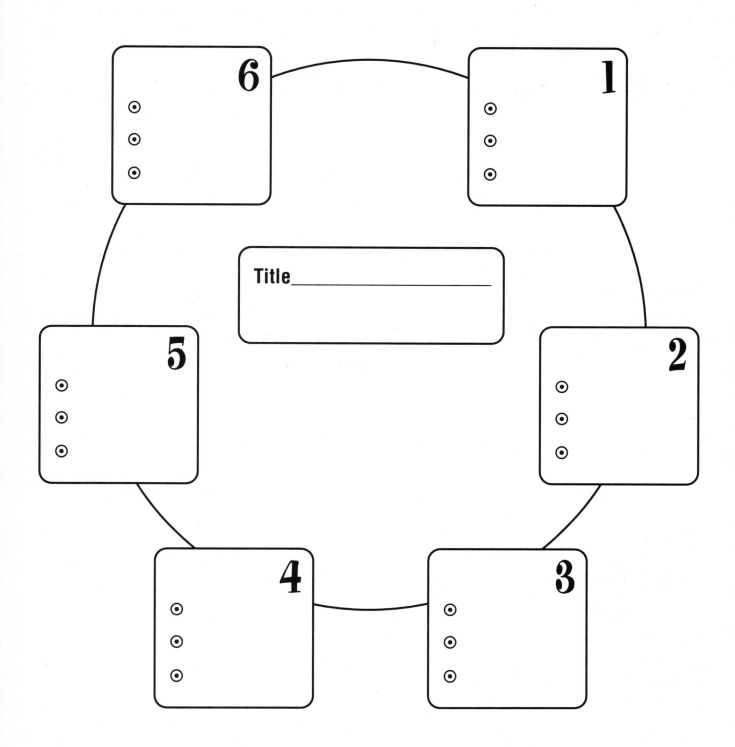

6

1

Title_____

5

2

4

3

Clock/Time Organizer

Description: This organizer helps students explore how they spend their time. By charting the time they spend on various activities, they can become better decision-makers about using time wisely.

Procedures:

1. Ask students to keep a record of how they spend time. Activities may include: sleep, meals, school, homework, television, play, etc.

2. Discuss (or review) abbreviations for morning and evening.

3. Have students draw a line from the center of the clock to the time they begin and end each activity (a radius) on the template.

4. Students can record the name of the activity in that section of the clock.

5. Encourage students to discuss and evaluate how much time they spend on various activities and whether or not they would like to make any changes.

Variations:

⊙ Have students complete this exercise before and after a lesson or unit on time management.

⊙ Students can complete this exercise and then complete another template showing how they plan to spend their time in the future.

⊙ Ask students to imagine how someone their age who grew up in another historical period (or the future) would spend his or her time.

⊙ Tell students to examine how others use their time—for example, historical figures in social studies or those in various occupations in career studies.

⊙ Use the clock as the basis for a pie chart by omitting the numerals. Pie charts can be helpful for understanding fractions and sharing data.

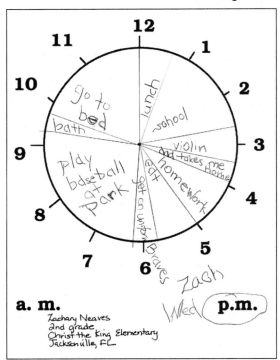

Zachery Neaves, a student in Kelly Gregory's class at Christ the King School in Jacksonville, Florida, used this organizer to show his use of time.

50 GRAPHIC ORGANIZERS FOR READING, WRITING, AND MORE
Scholastic Professional Books, 1999

Name_____ Date _____

Clock/Time Organizer

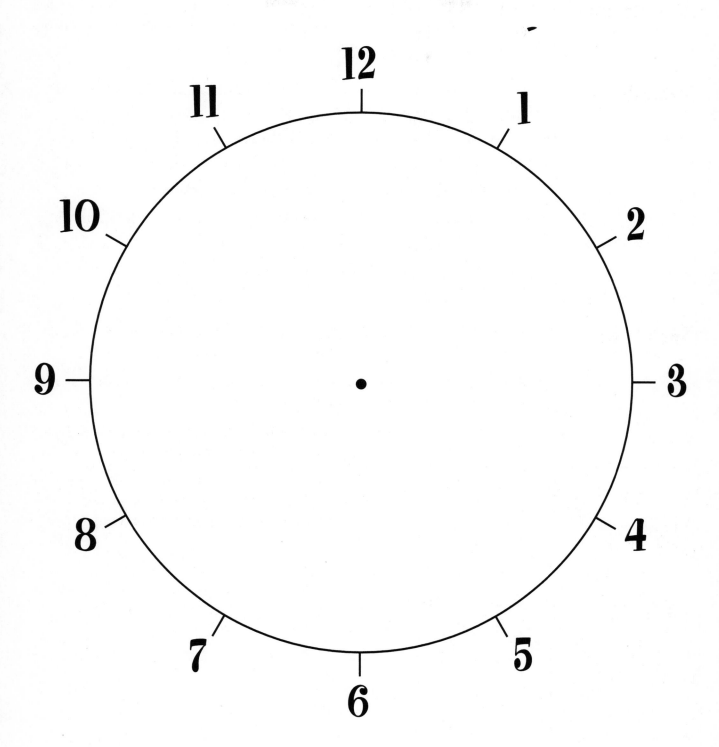

a.m.   p.m.

Coat of Arms Map

Description: This organizer is a good way for students to introduce themselves to one another. It emphasizes students' strengths and the positive things in their lives. The organizer supports a positive self-image and self-esteem.

Procedures:

1. Have students fill in their names in the bottom section of the template.

2. Ask students to think about each of the sections of the template and then fill in the information about themselves. The information can be written in or it can be represented by drawings or icons.

3. Encourage students to use color, drawings, and symbols and to be creative in completing the coat of arms.

4. Let students share the information with a partner or a small group so that they become comfortable talking about their individual coat of arms.

5. Have students share their coat of arms with the entire class.

Variations:

⊙ Complete templates for historical and fictional characters and give evidence for choices from the text.

⊙ Use the template to introduce concepts dealing with noble families and clans and the history of the coat of arms.

⊙ Omit the name from the bottom of the coat of arms and have students try and guess the identity of the person from the rest of the categories.

⊙ Change the categories to reflect students' ancestry: place of birth, ethnicity, and family history.

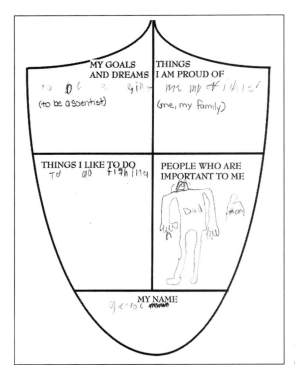

George, a fifth-grader in an inclusive classroom, created his coat of arms in Tracy D'Arpino's class at C. Fred Johnson Middle School in Johnson City, New York.

Coat of Arms Map

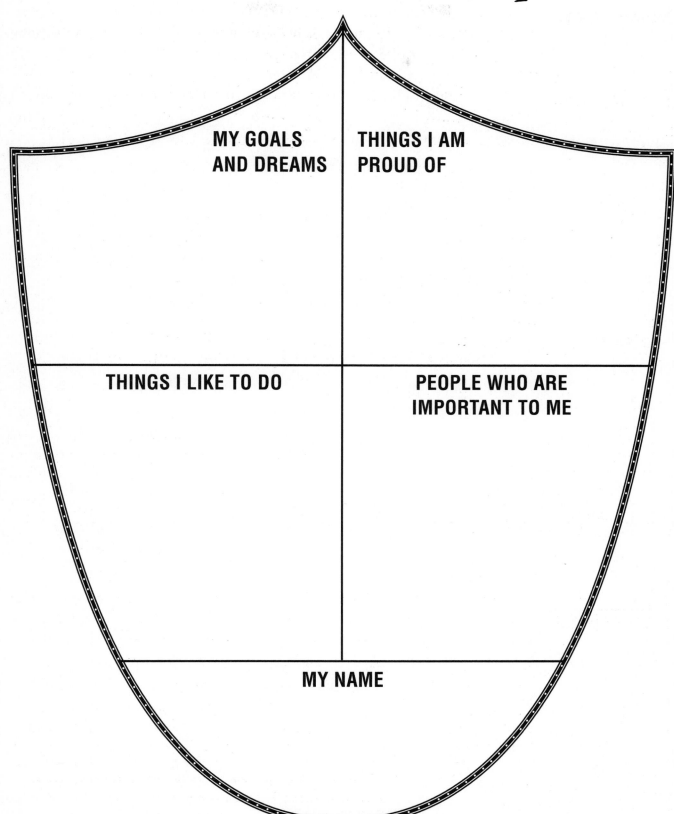

MY GOALS
AND DREAMS

THINGS I AM
PROUD OF

THINGS I LIKE TO DO

PEOPLE WHO ARE
IMPORTANT TO ME

MY NAME

Concept Definition Map

Description: Concept definition mapping, developed by Schwartz and Raphael (1985), focuses students' attention on the main components of a definition: the class or category, properties or characteristics, and illustrations or examples. As a strategy, it not only enriches students' understandings of a word or concept but also encourages them to integrate their personal knowledge into the definition.

Procedures:

1. Display the template on a chart or overhead projector.

2. Point out the questions that a complete definition answers, for example, *What is it? What is it like? What are some examples?*

3. Use a concept familiar to students and model how to complete the template. Demonstrate how to use information from subject-area readings, glossaries, or dictionaries and their own prior knowledge to complete the template.

4. Present a new term or concept from a subject or content area currently under study.

5. Ask students to work in pairs to write a definition of the new concept.

6. Have students read aloud or share the definition they wrote.

7. Evaluate the completeness of the definition by making sure it includes a class or category, properties or characteristics, and illustrations or examples.

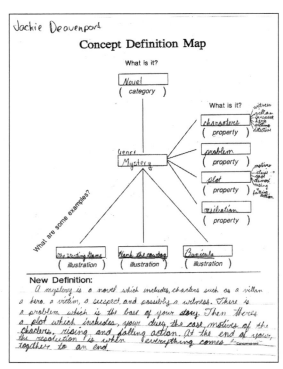

Variations:

⊙ Ask students to relate how their background knowledge helps them to write a complete definition.

⊙ Form cooperative groups and assign different terms or concepts to each group. Use these completed maps as a review or study guide for tests.

⊙ Play a mix-and-match game with students by eliminating the term or concept from the template. Have students identify the term or concept by reading the definition and the boxes in the template.

Jackie Deavenport in Kathy Buckner's fourth-grade class at Wilkerson Intermediate School in The Woodlands, Texas, created this map to clarify her understanding of the concept "mystery."

Concept Definition Map

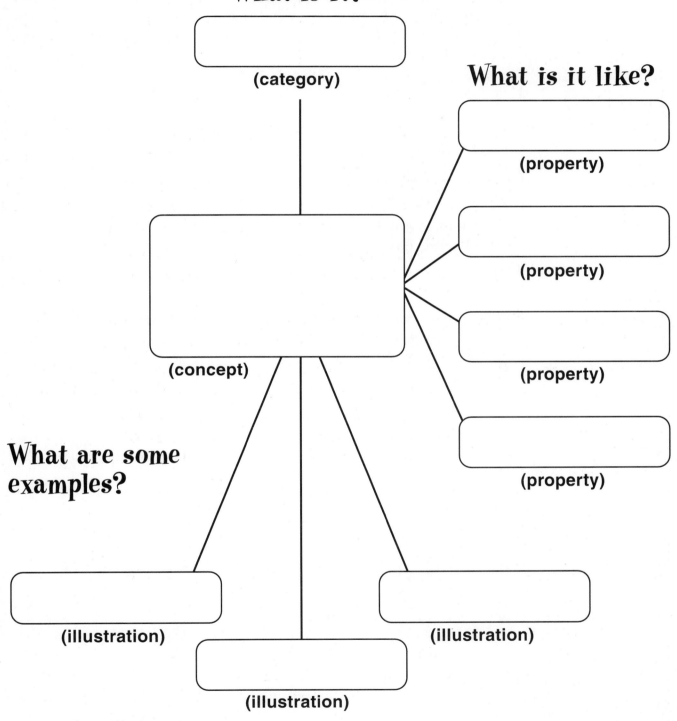

What is it?

(category)

What is it like?

(property)

(property)

(property)

(property)

(concept)

What are some examples?

(illustration)

(illustration)

(illustration)

New Definition: _____

_____

Data Chart

Description: A data chart is a grid on which information is organized into different categories. It is useful as a research tool because it allows students to compare categories of information using key variables or questions. This format makes it easy to see patterns in the data so students can generate hypotheses or explore categories of information.

Procedures:

1. Work with students to choose a subject to research.

2. Brainstorm topics or questions to explore about the subject and list them across the top of the template.

3. Brainstorm titles of resources to consult and list them vertically down the left side of the template.

4. Have students conduct research and/or search the various resources and fill in the boxes in the template with the appropriate information.

5. Then use the grid to launch a discussion or writing exercise.

Variations:

⊙ When the grid is complete, students can turn their notes into a research paper by making each of the columns a separate paragraph.

⊙ Have students use the data chart to record information as they interview one another to learn interviewing techniques. Put students' names down the left-hand column and questions across the top in the other columns.

⊙ Use a data chart to compare several versions of the same folktale, such as Cinderella tales.

⊙ Utilize the data chart to record observations during science experiments or to record the use of social skills by group members. Have students record exact words or gestures observed.

Rebecca Beers's class at Catawba Springs Elementary School in Belmont, North Carolina, made a number of data charts to support its unit on Mexico.

50 Graphic Organizers for Reading, Writing, and More
Scholastic Professional Books, 1999

Name_____ Date _____

Data Chart

Research Subject _____

Resources				TOPICS			

Discussion Web

Description: The discussion web (adapted by Alvermann (1991) from Duthie (1986)) helps students look at both sides of an issue before drawing conclusions. Discussion webs stimulate thinking and build on the notion that some of our best thinking results from a group's collective efforts. The strategy helps students develop the ability to listen, understand, accept other points of view, and enrich and refine their own understandings.

Procedures:

1. After reading a story or chapter from a content area textbook, discuss students' reactions and interpretations.

2. Identify an issue that is central to the reading and put it in the center square on the template in the form of a question.

3. Have students work in pairs to discuss the *yeses* and *nos* of the question and record their ideas in the appropriate boxes.

4. Pair one set of partners with another to compare answers as they work toward a yes or no conclusion(s).

5. Record the conclusion in the box at the bottom of the template. Have a spokesperson from each group use the template to explain its conclusion to the class.

6. Through discussion, try to arrive at a class conclusion.

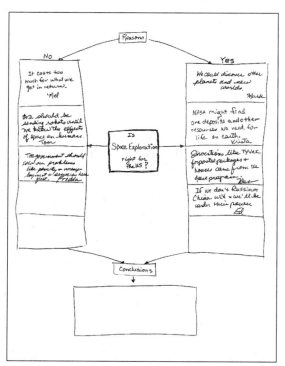

Variations:

⊙ Ask individuals to write their answers to the question. Post these responses in the classroom so students can read one another's ideas.

⊙ Use the activity across curriculum areas, for example, replace the *yes* and *no* with famous people and cite their views on a historical or social issue (Mark Twain and Mildred Taylor on slavery, for example).

⊙ Use the discussion web as a prereading activity to assess and organize prior knowledge and then use as a postreading activity to show students how new information can change thinking.

This partially completed web shows the reasons for and against U.S. space exploration. Students will do research, debate the issues, and then complete the conclusions section.

36

Name_____ Date _____

Discussion Web

REASONS YES

REASONS NO

THE CENTRAL QUESTION

CONCLUSIONS

Feature Matrix

Description: A feature matrix is a table that allows students to compare the characteristics of several different things. Since it contains information that has been organized into categories, it is a quick way to interpret a large quantity of data and see patterns of similarity and difference.

Procedures:

1. Label the matrix at the top of the page.

2. Identify the things or objects to be compared and write them in the column down the left side of the template.

3. Note the characteristics to be compared and write each in one of the rows across the top of the template.

4. Determine whether each object listed in the column has any of the characteristics listed in the rows, and if there is a match, place an *X* in the box.

5. Continue to evaluate and mark each object in the column.

6. Look for similarities by noting patterns of *X*'s and look for differences by noting blank boxes.

7. Encourage students to discuss similarities and differences and draw conclusions.

Variations:

- Use in math to determine the processes (algorithms) needed to solve problems.

- Depending on their age or developmental stage, have students use + or -, *Y* or *N*, or other brief notations instead of *X*'s.

- Have students use colored pens or pencils so patterns in the data emerge more easily.

- Ask students to record information during a science experiment so it is easier to form a hypothesis.

Vertebrates

	Cold-blooded	warm-blooded	feathers	lays eggs	hair	scales	backbone	lungs	
reptiles	X			X		X	X	X	
mammals		X	placentas		X		X	X	
amphibians	X						X	X	
birds		X	X	X			X	X	
fish	X			X			X	X	

Elsa Bingel and Deborah Griesinger worked with their students in a multiage classroom at Tioga Hills Elementary School in Vestal, New York, to create this matrix comparing characteristics of different vertebrates.

50 GRAPHIC ORGANIZERS FOR READING, WRITING, AND MORE
Scholastic Professional Books, 1999

Name_____ Date _____

Feature Matrix

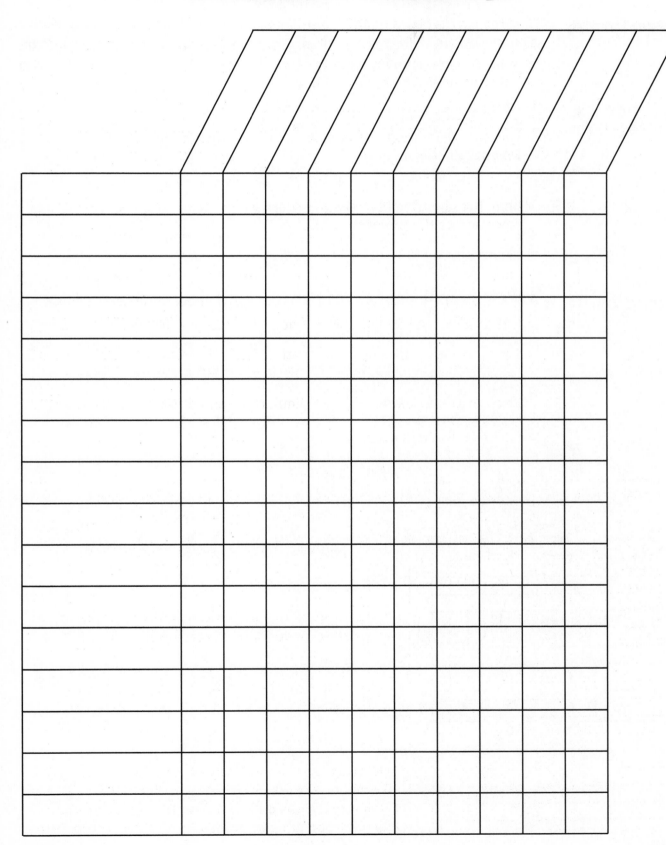

Finding Math Factors Organizer

Description: This organizer is designed to help students understand the various factors that can make up any given number. It is important for students to understand the associative and commutative properties of numbers.

Procedures:

1. Discuss the concept of factors in mathematics.

2. Have students write the number to be factored in the circle in the middle of the template.

3. Ask students to write all of the possible factors of the number in the boxes. Add or delete boxes as necessary.

4. Discuss the commutative property of numbers using the completed organizer.

Variations:

⊙ Let students brainstorm all of the possible number addition (or subtraction) equations that can equal the number in the circle. Put an equation in each box.

⊙ Have students having difficulty use manipulatives to complete the organizer.

⊙ Compare organizers to show the difference between numbers that can be factored and prime numbers.

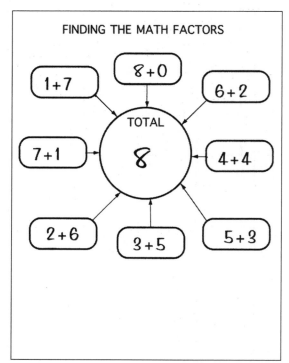

This organizer for the factors of 8 was done on the computer.

50 GRAPHIC ORGANIZERS FOR READING, WRITING, AND MORE
Scholastic Professional Books, 1999

Name_____   Date _____

Finding Math Factors
Organizer

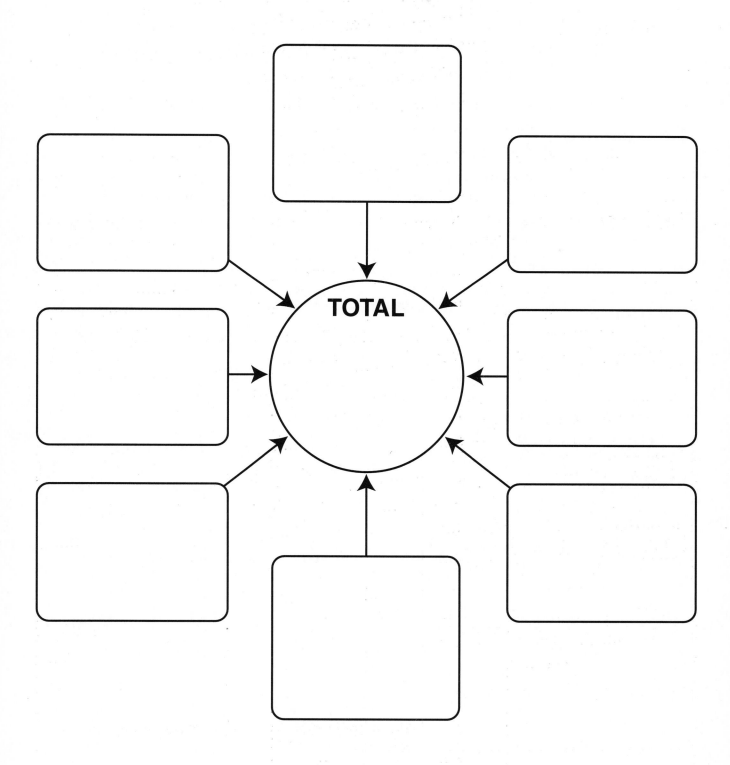

TOTAL

Getting Into Character Map

Description: Following or during reading, this map is used to represent and analyze the various feelings, thoughts, and actions of a character in a story. Creating this type of map helps learners feel and think like the character to better understand the range of a character's emotions and behaviors.

Procedures:

1. Urge students to imagine how it feels to be the character by standing in his or her shoes.

2. After or during reading, discuss the character's feelings, thoughts, and actions.

3. Record these in the appropriate places on the template.

4. Ask students to think about possible reasons for certain actions and identify relationships among feelings, thoughts, and actions.

5. Discuss the character as a whole person, helping students analyze and understand the motivations and complex internal and external interactions that make up a personality.

Variations:

⊙ Do a template for a character after the first chapter in a book and at the end of the book. Compare and contrast templates to identify areas of character growth and change.

⊙ Use this with students to introduce each other at the beginning of the year or when you form new cooperative groups as a way to get to know one another.

⊙ The Getting Into Character template can become a blueprint for writing a character sketch or doing a character analysis for a book report.

⊙ Use in science or social studies to help students better understand a historical character or real person who lived in a different time period or place, perhaps using past tense verbs such as *saw, heard, smelled, said, thought…*

⊙ Put exact quotes from the text on the template to show how authors use language to depict emotions.

Domenica Cerasaro, a fifth grader at T. J. Watson Elementary School in Endicott, New York, created this map on Tony Souza, a character in Windcatcher *by Avi.*

Name Domenica   Date May 11

Getting Into Character Map

Character Tony
Book Title Windcatcher
Author Avi

thinks
about the treasure
about the snark

hears
Grandma's warnings
about the water

smells
clams, salt water

sees
the statue of Captain
Little John
the thimble islands

says
wants to sail
alone

does
- explores
- gets people
worried about him

does
goes sailing

loves
- to sail in the
Snark
- money

feels
- mad at the couple
- scared of the couple
- eager to find the
treasure

goes
Grandma's house
near Long Island
Sound

goes
Sailing to the
Statue

50 Graphic Organizers for Reading, Writing, and More
Scholastic Professional Books, 1999   48

Name_____   Date _____

Getting Into Character Map

Character _____

Book Title _____

Author _____

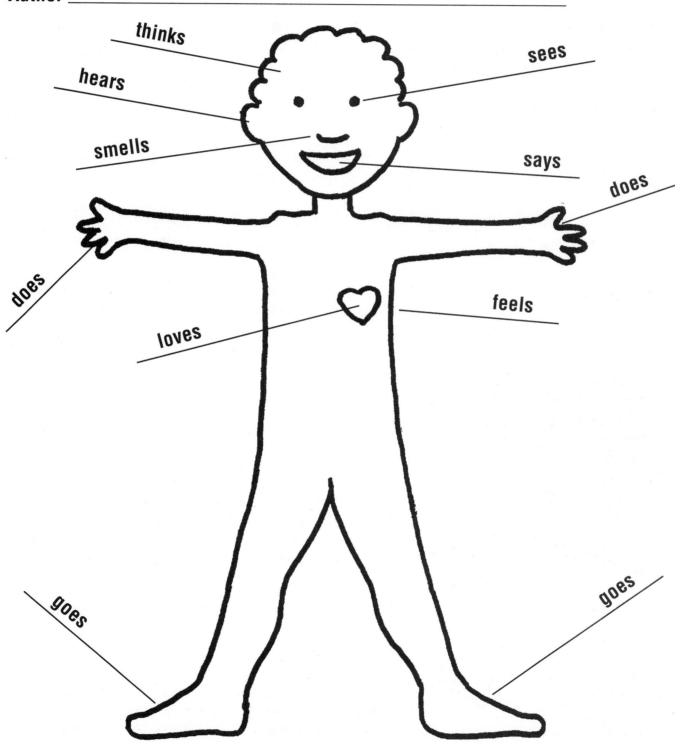

thinks

sees

hears

smells

says

does

does

feels

loves

goes

goes

Hierarchical Organizer

Description: This organizer helps students to see superordinate and subordinate categories or ranks of a main topic or concept. The important aspect of this type of organization is that there are distinct levels or ranks that proceed from top to bottom because of importance or level of abstraction. This organizer clarifies relationships between and among the ranks or levels. Anything that is set up in a ranking of categories and subcategories can be depicted in a hierarchical organizer.

Procedures:

1. Have students choose the topic for the organizer and record it in the diamond at the top of the template. The topic should be one with which you and your students are familiar.

2. Ask students to brainstorm a list of the subcategories of the topic.

3. Students should cluster the ideas on the list into ranks, levels, or subcategories and determine the number of ranks or levels.

4. Have students write the first subdivisions in the boxes in the level just below the main idea. Add or delete boxes as needed.

5. Have students put the subdivisions of each box in the circles below it. Add or delete circles as needed.

6. With material that has four or more ranks, the students will need to add additional levels. You might use triangles to represent the fourth level.

Variations:

⊙ Use fewer levels with younger students.

⊙ Fill in some of the boxes at each level to help students who are unfamiliar with the topic or this type of organizational pattern.

⊙ Fill in the lowest rank and have students brainstorm the higher classifications and categories.

⊙ Provide the words for the organizer in random order and let students complete the organizer. This can be done with 3- by 5-inch index cards so that students can rearrange them on the floor or on a bulletin board.

At St. James Middle School in Binghamton, New York, Greg Lehr's eighth-grade social studies students created graphic organizers during their study of the Industrial Revolution.

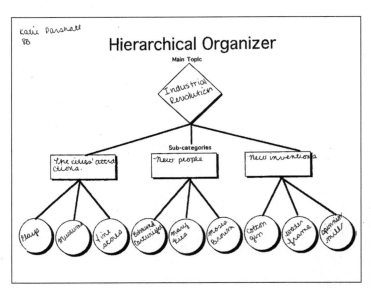

50 Graphic Organizers for Reading, Writing, and More
Scholastic Professional Books, 1999

Name_____ Date _____

Hierarchical Organizer

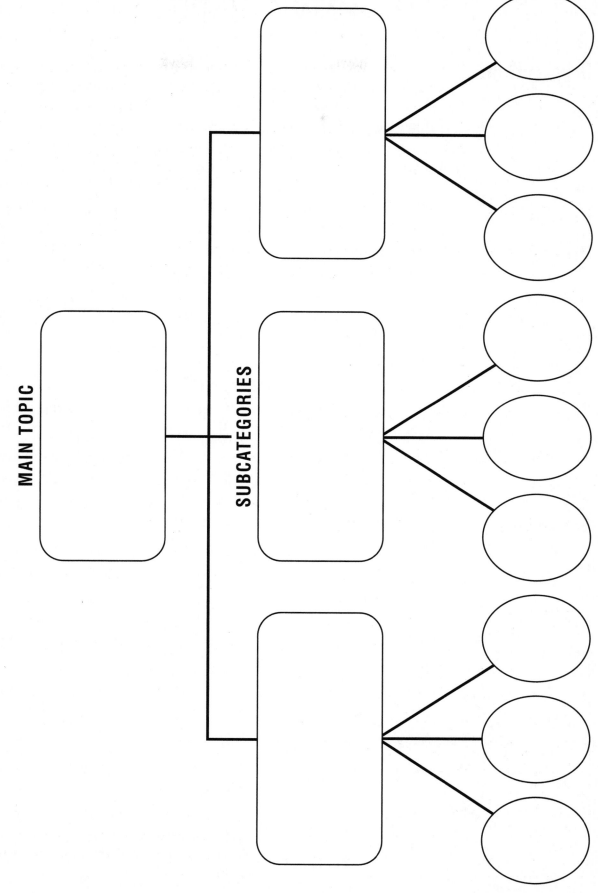

MAIN TOPIC

SUBCATEGORIES

Icon Map

Description: An icon is a symbol or picture that stands for a concept, idea, or object. As the saying "A picture is worth a thousand words" suggests, an icon often triggers more and different associations than a printed word. An icon map uses a picture to represent a central concept from which related ideas radiate. This map uses a "List, Group, Label" strategy (Readance, Bean and Baldwin, 1998) to help students differentiate between superordinate and subordinate ideas/main ideas and supporting details. Use this map with students who enjoy drawing or have trouble distinguishing main ideas and supporting details.

Procedures:

1. Choose a picture or symbol that is central to a reading selection or story and put it in the center of the template.

2. Brainstorm a list of issues, characteristics, or broad categories of information that relate to the icon.

3. Group similar words and ideas from the list together.

4. Draw an icon for each group and label it.

5. Record supporting information around each related icon.

Variations:

⊙ Use icon maps in science, social studies, and math as an effective way to conclude a unit or chapter study.

⊙ To stimulate interest and activate prior knowledge before reading a story, provide students with an icon that is central to the story and brainstorm related ideas.

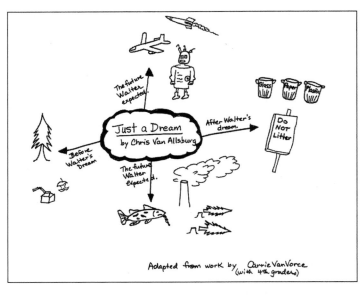

Carrie Van Vorce worked with fourth graders to create an icon map based on Just a Dream *by Chris Van Allsburg.*

Name_____ Date _____

Icon Map

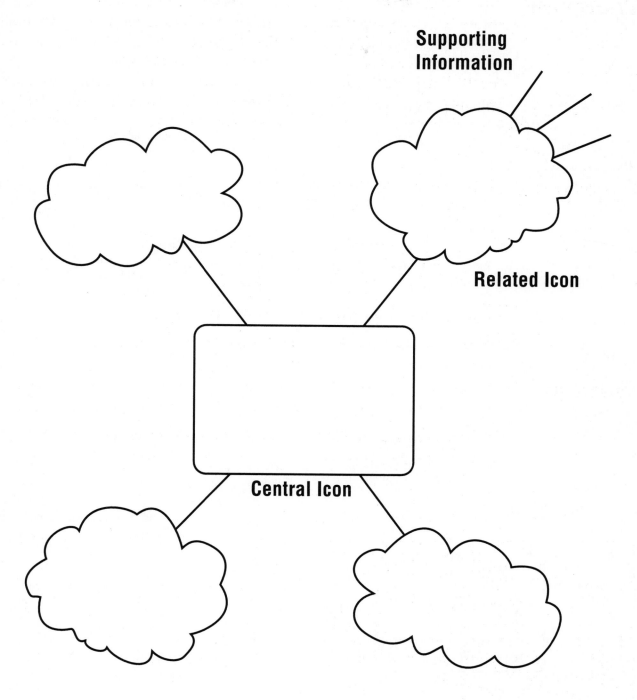

Supporting
Information

Related Icon

Central Icon

K-W-L Chart

Description: A K-W-L (Ogle, 1986) chart helps students understand what they *know* (**K**), what they *want to know* (**W**), and what they *learned* (**L**) when reading or researching a topic. This is an effective visual tool to involve students by tapping their prior knowledge and letting them set their own purposes for learning. By analyzing the **L** column, both the teacher and students can evaluate students' grasp of knowledge or content. Then the teacher can make plans to enrich concepts or to remedy misconceptions.

Procedures:

1. Construct the organizer and preteach or review the terms on the template.

2. Write the information the students brainstorm about the topic in the **K** (know) column.

3. Record the questions the students have about the topic in the **W** (want to know) column. This establishes a purpose for reading or researching.

4. After the students have read, researched, and discussed the topic, place the new information in the **L** (learned) column.

5. Discuss with students whether they can now confirm or deny any statements listed in the **K** column.

Variations:

⊙ Create a **K-W-H-L** chart, adding the **H** for ***How** I will learn.*

⊙ Add an **S** after **K-W-L** for *what I **Still** want to learn.*

⊙ Use a **K-T-W-L** when students ***Think*** they know (**T**) information but are not positive.

⊙ Introduce in science, social studies, and math as a prereading, during reading, and postreading strategy.

⊙ Incorporate K-W-L in students' learning logs or journal-writing activities.

⊙ Use K-W-L when viewing videos, preparing for guest speakers, or going on a field trip.

⊙ Employ K-W-L as a guide for computer-researched projects.

A group of 4 eighth graders at Vestal Middle School in Vestal, New York, and their teacher, Colleen Schultz, created this K-W-H-L chart on "Real Numbers."

50 GRAPHIC ORGANIZERS FOR READING, WRITING, AND MORE
Scholastic Professional Books, 1999

Name_____ Date _____

K-W-L Chart

K What (I) we know	W What (I) we want to find out	L What (I) we learned

Main Idea Pyramid Organizer

Description: This organizer displays the various levels of details that support the main idea. This organizer can be used to examine the structure of a paragraph or longer text. It may also be used to help students organize details and evidence to support a main idea or a conclusion.

Procedures:

1. Decide upon a topic or main idea. Write the topic in the box at the top of the main idea pyramid.

2. In the box underneath, write an explanation or a brief paraphrase of the main idea.

3. In the next four boxes, write four supporting ideas.

4. Underneath each of the four boxes, write the details and/or examples that support the ideas.

5. You may wish to modify the last two levels by including more or fewer boxes as needed.

6. Use the completed pyramid as a guide for writing or discussing the main idea and the quality of the evidence or supporting details.

Variations:

⊙ Have students begin at the lowest level of detail or evidence and generate the main idea.

⊙ Use the pyramid to examine the evidence for a particular idea or conclusion, or break down the steps and processes needed for a project.

⊙ Suggest that students put a personal goal in the top box and use the supporting levels to document what and how they will achieve the goal.

⊙ Highlight a classification such as *insect*, a definition, the main characteristics, and examples.

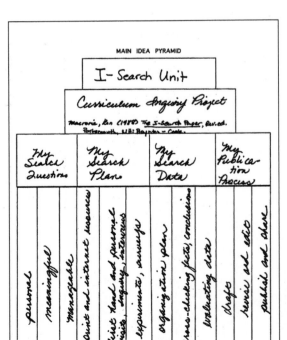

The concept of this organizer was adapted from an article by J. Zorfass, published in 1994, "Supporting students with learning disabilities: Integrating technology into an I-Search unit." Technology and Disability, 3 (2), 129–136. The organizer presents students' plans for their I-Search research project.

Main Idea Pyramid Organizer

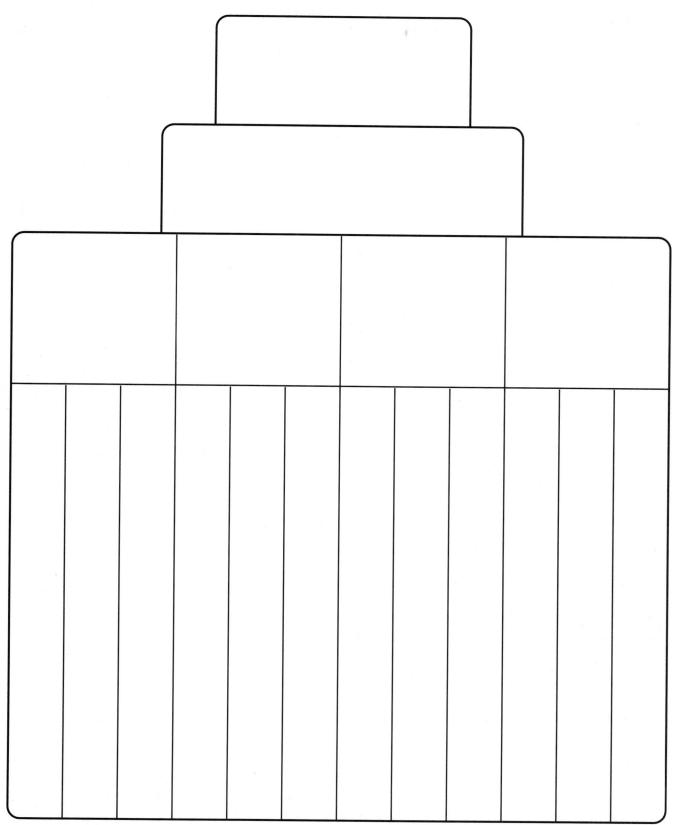

Math Sentences Organizer

Description: This organizer helps students to see all of the different number sentences (equations) that can equal one number. Because the organizer includes addition, subtraction, multiplication, and division, it facilitates an understanding of the relationship of these basic math concepts.

Procedures:

1. Decide upon a number to put in the central square.

2. Begin with the bottom section, marked addition, and brainstorm with students all of the number sentences that equal the number in the middle square.

3. Repeat this process for the subtraction, multiplication, and division sections.

Variations:

⊙ Put a money amount (such as $1.00) in the center box and change each symbol to the name of a coin (penny, nickel, dime, quarter). Have students calculate the number of coins of each type that equal the amount in the middle.

⊙ For older students, put a symbol (x) in the box, and have them generate equations in each of the quadrants whose answer equals the symbol in the box, for example, (x+y)-y=___.

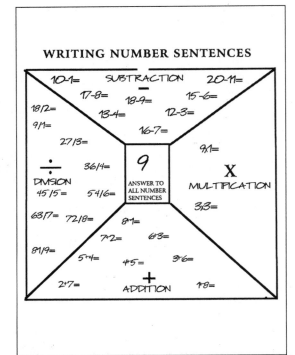

This organizer illustrates the number sentences for the number 9. It was created on a computer.

Name_____ Date _____

Math Sentences Organizer

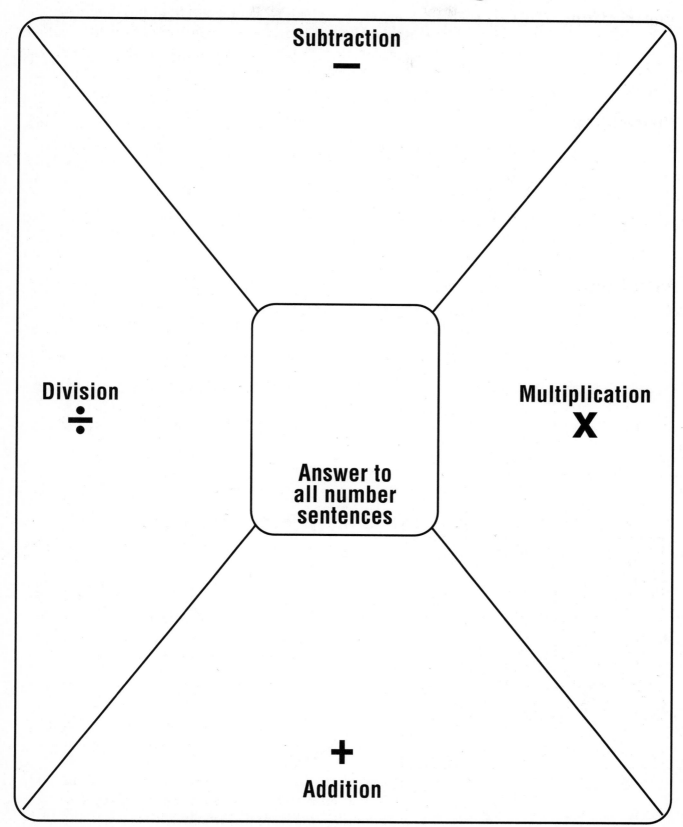

Subtraction

–

Division

÷

Answer to all number sentences

Multiplication

X

+

Addition

Mind Map

Description: A mind map by Buzan (1995) is a brainstorming tool that uses colors and pictures (icons) to symbolize key concepts. The combination of colors and pictures produces more associations than do words. It is particularly effective for visual and nontraditional learners.

Procedures:

1. Choose a topic.

2. Create a picture or icon that represents the topic.

3. Add the topic to the center of the map.

4. Brainstorm related concepts, examples, and feelings.

5. Use different colors or pictures to group or identify related ideas.

6. Add connector lines and key words.

Variations:

⊙ Use words to describe relationships among concepts. Label connector lines with verbs to describe the relation or connection.

⊙ Draw different kinds of lines (dotted, or heavy arrows, for example) to show different types of relationships or connections.

⊙ Provide the central skeleton of a mind map and have individuals or small groups complete their own maps and explain their rationale to the larger group.

⊙ Encourage all students to participate by giving everyone a different colored pen so that individual contributions are clear.

⊙ A teacher-created mind map can be used as a unit overview.

⊙ Use butcher paper to create an ongoing mind map as a unit progresses. Encourage students to add to it with markers or stick-on notes. This connects daily lessons to each other and can serve as a review tool.

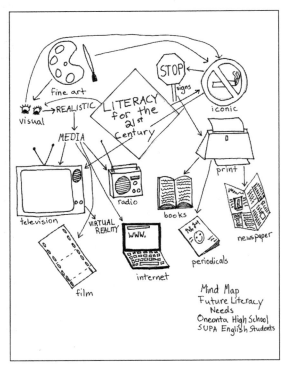

This map was created by Katie Alex, Tracy Shaw, Leigh Irwin, and Jen Horne, SUPA English students at Oneonta High School, Oneonta, New York. This group brainstormed the literacy needs for students in the next century and created this organizer using the flow chart commands in Mighty Draw Software.

Name_____ Date _____

Mind Map

Use drawings, icons, colors, and/or words to show the ideas and associations you have for a concept.

Multiple Intelligence Planner

Description: This organizer is designed to facilitate curricular planning using the multiple intelligence model developed by Howard Gardner (1993; 1997). Gardner theorizes that there are eight intelligences: spatial, bodily-kinesthetic, musical, linguistic, logical-mathematical, interpersonal, intrapersonal, and naturalistic, which Gardner has recently added to his theory. The template may be used by a teacher, a team of teachers, or by a teacher with students.

Procedures:

1. Decide upon a topic or theme that will be the organizing focus of the unit or project and record it in the circle at the center of the template. Record the learning objectives for the unit or project below the web on the template.

2. Review and discuss the various types of intelligences that are included in the Gardner model.

3. Brainstorm the types of meaningful activities related to the topic that draw upon each of the eight types of intelligences. Record the activities in the appropriate part of the web.

4. Evaluate and discuss the balance of activities as they relate to the learning objectives recorded on the template. Modify, delete, or add activities to facilitate the objectives. Remember that there does not have to be an equal balance among the activities for each type of intelligence. Some topics will naturally favor one or more of the types of intelligence.

Note: Do not forget that the assessment of learning should also reflect the various intelligences.

Variations:

⊙ When planning with a team or group, decide which members will prepare each set of activities.

⊙ In a departmental situation, include the various subjects and teachers responsible for each activity.

⊙ Use the template to profile individuals according to the eight intelligences.

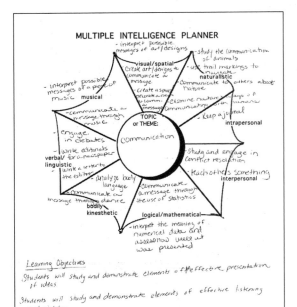

Jennifer Sharples, a practicum student at Binghamton University, used this organizer to plan for a seventh-grade language arts class.

Name_____ Date _____

Multiple Intelligence Planner

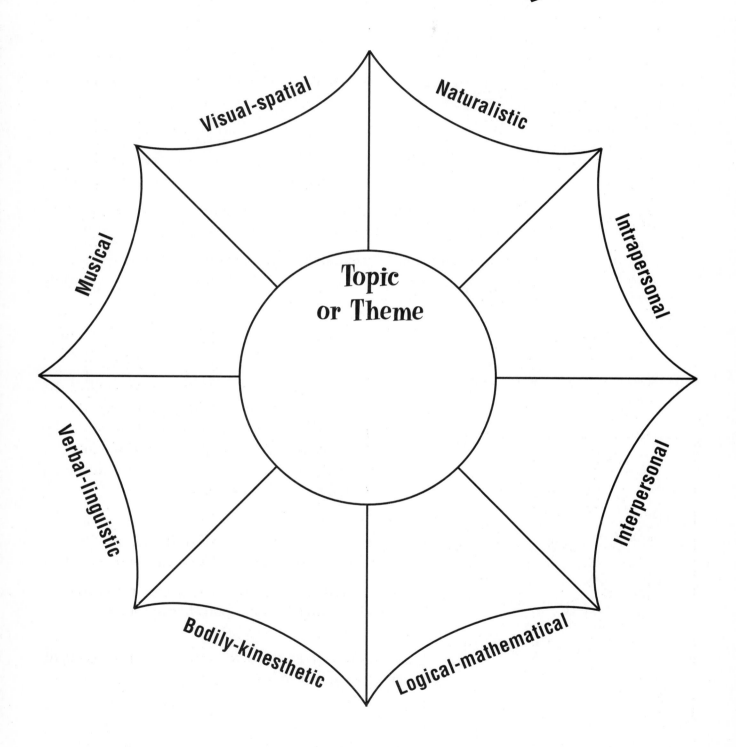

Multiple Meaning Map

Description: A multiple meaning map helps students explore words with more than one meaning. It includes various meanings, definitions, examples, and associations. Both pictures and print are used to extend the learner's vocabulary by creating associations and conceptual links.

Procedures:

1. Print a word with multiple meanings in the center rectangle on the template.

2. Ask students for various meanings of the word, and discuss these ideas to help students make connections.

3. Write these words in the triangles on the template (adding or deleting triangles as needed).

4. Write each word's definition on the line connecting it to the central word.

5. Brainstorm students' associations for each word.

6. Write these ideas around each word, drawing pictures to illustrate concepts.

7. Then have students use dictionaries, thesauruses, textbook glossaries, or other references to find new meanings for the word and add this information to the map.

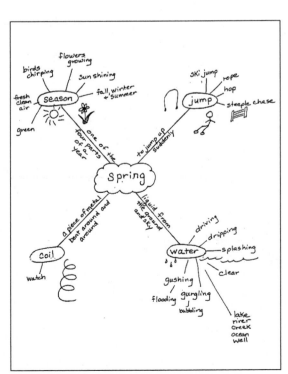

Variations:

- Use in science, social studies, health, and math to help students understand that technical words can have multiple meanings.

- Form small cooperative groups and assign a different word to each group. Then have each group teach its word to the class.

- With linguistically diverse students, record the various translations (Spanish, Chinese, etc.) as well as the English words.

Note: For ESL learners, these explicit discussions of multiple meanings and connotations are important in helping them acquire conventional English.

Linda Hopkins's class at Tioga Hills School in the Vestal Central School District in New York, created this map.

50 Graphic Organizers for Reading, Writing, and More
Scholastic Professional Books, 1999

Multiple Meaning Map

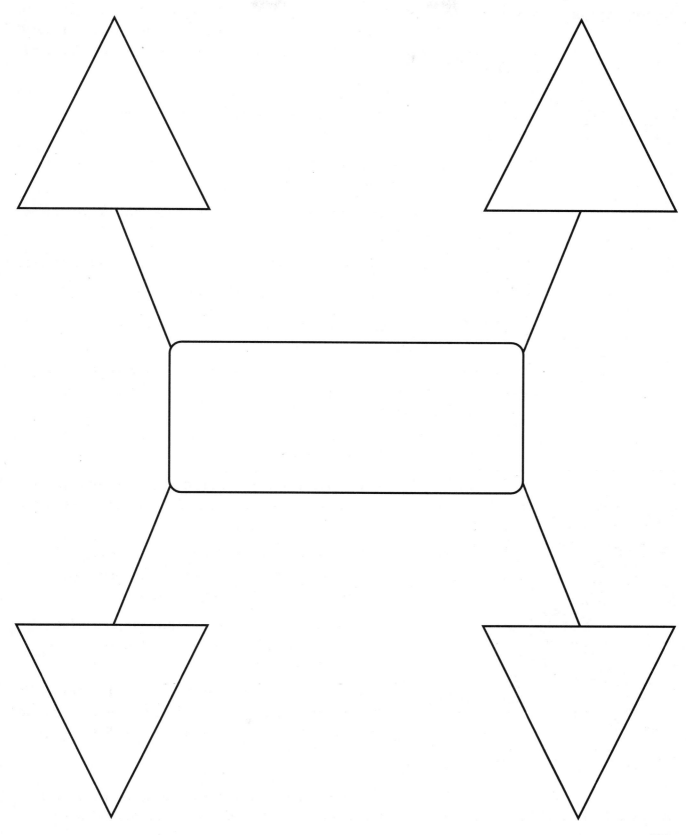

Multiple Timeline

Description: This variation on a simple timeline allows students to look at various aspects of a time period and see the influences they have on one another. For instance, a class might trace the political events, the economic events, and the cultural milestones of the 1920s in America, or a student could compare the inventions in America, Great Britain, and Germany during the 1940s.

Procedures:

1. Give or negotiate with your students the topic of the multiple timeline and enter it at the top of the template.

2. Have students enter the beginning and ending years covered by the timeline in the appropriate blanks on the template.

3. Decide upon which subtopics or aspects you and/or your students wish to include on the template and put one on each line.

4. Have individuals or groups read and research to find the dates and key events that fit each subtopic or aspect. Have students enter them on or below the appropriate lines.

5. Conclude by having students discuss as a class or in smaller groups the various subtopics and aspects and their relationships to form a better understanding of the time period.

Variations:

- Use pictures or icons, rather than words, to illustrate the events that occurred and their dates.

- Compare the key events in the lives of three presidents, three authors, or three typical children from different countries or cultures during a specific time.

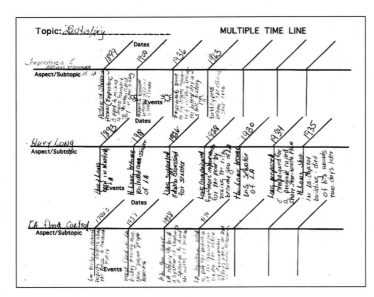

- Add lines for additional aspects/subtopics.

- Have students use the template to compare key events in their lives.

- Use the timelines to make predictions on various aspects of life in the future.

Eighth graders at St. Charles Borromeo School in Destrehan, Louisiana, worked with their teacher, Pat Lynch, to create this multiple timeline on various aspects of Louisiana history.

Name_____ Date _____

Multiple Timeline

TOPIC:

Dates | Events | Aspect/Subtopic

Dates | Events | Aspect/Subtopic

Dates | Events | Aspect/Subtopic

One and All Organizer

Description: One and All is a framework for uncovering similarities and differences among four items. Developed by Karen and Wayne Trainer, this organizer is also known as "windows" or "uncommon commonalities" (Kagan, 1994). One and All focuses on comparing and contrasting items.

Procedures:

1. Identify the general topic to be compared.

2. Give each student a number (1, 2, 3, 4) and a subtopic.

3. Model by using a characteristic that is true for all subtopics, and place in the **ALL** space. If a characteristic is only true for one of the subtopics, place it in the appropriate number space.

4. Have students name a trait of their subtopic. Decide if that trait is unique, or if it is shared.

5. Record shared traits in the circle **ALL**, and the unique traits in the outer boxes (1, 2, 3, 4).

6. Ask students to give the rationale for their decisions.

Variations:

⊙ Have students work in collaborative groups to discuss where items should be placed on the template.

⊙ Prewrite book titles or characters from a book on the template prior to sharing it with students.

⊙ As a team-builder, have students place items which are common to the team in the center of the template, and place items true of each individual in the outside segments.

⊙ One and All can be used in social studies (for example, to compare countries), or in science (to compare plants).

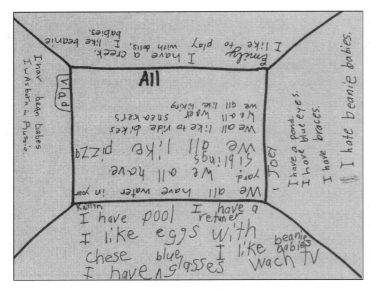

Small groups in Karen Wassell's class at Vestal Hills Elementary School in Vestal, New York, used this organizer to build a sense of community by sharing things that they had in common and ways in which they were different.

Name_____ Date _____

One and All Organizer

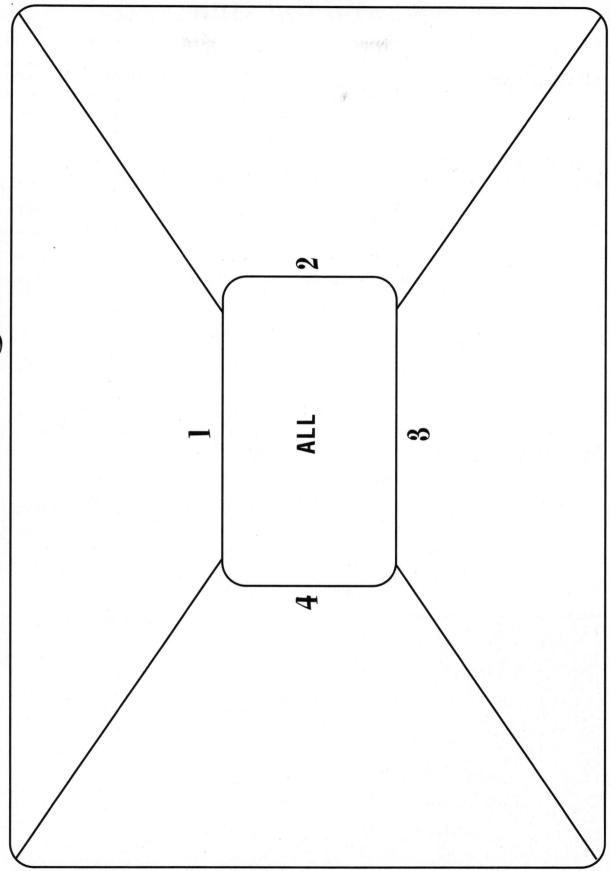

1

2

ALL

3

4

50 GRAPHIC ORGANIZERS FOR READING, WRITING, AND MORE
Scholastic Professional Books, 1999

Pictograph

Description: The pictograph helps students make comparisons understand proportion, percentages, and fractions. The pictures (icons) help students understand the ways in which data can be depicted visually.

Procedures:

1. Have students decide what types of information they are going to count and compare. Choose a title and record it in the appropriate blank.

2. Decide upon the drawing or symbol that will represent the item(s) and the number of units represented. Put the symbol(s) and number(s) in the KEY box at the bottom of the template.

3. Have students decide how many symbols are needed to represent each category and draw them in the appropriate row. The third row may be used to show the total.

4. When the pictograph is complete, have students determine the percentages of the total. Record in the box at the end of each row.

Variations:

⊙ Implement the pictograph to practice fractions by letting the number of items in a row be the numerator and the total number of items be the denominator.

⊙ Let students use clip art and do the pictograph on the computer.

⊙ Use different symbols in each row to represent the products of a country, demographic categories, or scientific population counts of various plants and animals.

This pictograph shows the student population of Oneonta, New York.

50 Graphic Organizers for Reading, Writing, and More
Scholastic Professional Books, 1999

Pictograph

TITLE: _____

Categories	Symbols	Percentage

KEY

Item 1 | Item 2 | Item 3

Symbol = number of units

Plot Diagram

Description: The plot diagram helps students summarize and illustrate the plot of any story. Students can depict their understanding of the events of the story by supplying statements for the terms *introduction*, *rising action*, *falling action*, and *resolution*.

Procedures:

1. Read the story and discuss students' interpretations and responses.

2. Construct the diagram and preteach or review the terms on the template.

3. Discuss the important events from the story.

4. Brainstorm this list on a chart.

5. Model, using an overhead transparency or large chart, how to write a concise summary statement for each event.

6. Work with students to place these statements on the plot diagram.

7. Add pictures or icons on the template where appropriate.

Variations:

⊙ Use this organizer as a postreading tool to assess students' comprehension of a story.

⊙ Provide pictures or icons to replace the written summary statements. Students must be able to justify their icons by referring to specific events in the story.

⊙ Students may work in cooperative groups to develop one plot diagram. They will experience the value of negotiation as they attempt to reach consensus on important events.

⊙ Change terms to synonyms that are developmentally appropriate for older students, for example, *introduction* to *exposition*, *resolution* to *denouement*.

⊙ Use the plot diagram as the basis for retelling a story or writing a summary.

⊙ Use the plot diagram to plan a story, script, or video creation.

Megan, a student in Sarah Evans's sixth-grade language arts class, created this plot diagram based upon The Adventures of Tom Sawyer *by Mark Twain. Sarah teaches at Vestal Middle School in Vestal, New York.*

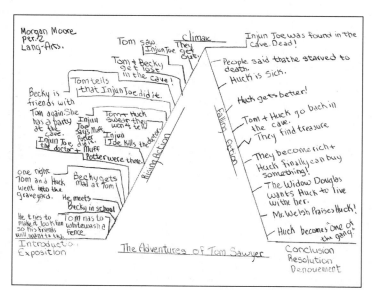

50 Graphic Organizers for Reading, Writing, and More
Scholastic Professional Books, 1999

Plot Diagram

Climax

Falling Action

Resolution

Rising Action

Introduction

50 GRAPHIC ORGANIZERS FOR READING, WRITING, AND MORE
Scholastic Professional Books, 1999

Read/View/Compare Map

Description: This organizer helps students compare a book and video/movie according to several criteria. It can be used to record a discussion of the book and video/movie or as a planning and organizing tool for comparison.

Procedures:

1. Identify a story that is in both book and video/movie form.

2. Have students read the book and view the video/movie.

3. On the template, write the title of the book on the book icon and the title of the movie on the camera icon.

4. Lead students in a discussion of similarities and differences between the book and video/movie.

5. Record information on the appropriate lines on the template, for example, put information about characters in the book on the line originating from the book and information about characters in the video/movie on the line originating from the camera, etc.

Variations:

⊙ Produce a template with two book icons to compare two versions of the same story, for example, Cinderella variants like *Yeh-Shen: A Cinderella Story from China* retold by Ai-Ling Louie and *The Rough-Face Girl* (Native American) by Rafe Martin, or two books by the same author, (*Bridge to Terabithia* and *Park's Quest* by Katherine Paterson).

⊙ Create a template with two camera icons to compare two movies about the same topic.

⊙ Use the template to plan a movie, multimedia presentation, or play based upon a book. (Some of the criteria may remain the same, but others may vary.)

⊙ Utilize the template to plan an updated version of a classic story.

Janelle L. Billings, a graduate student at Binghamton University, created this map comparing the book and movie versions of Pocahontas.

Read/View/Compare

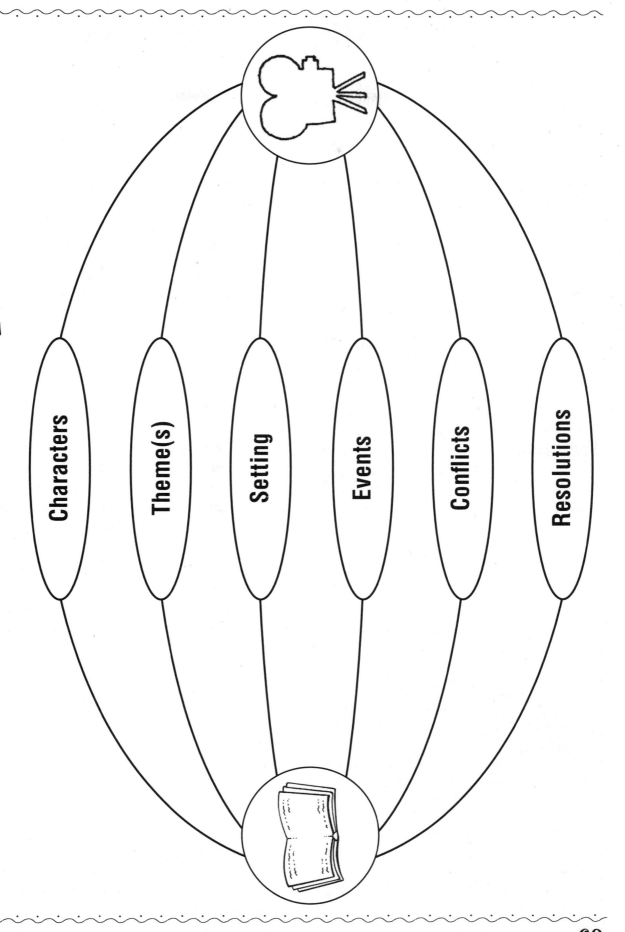

Characters

Theme(s)

Setting

Events

Conflicts

Resolutions

See Shell Category Map

Description: The See Shell helps students identify a category or class and the examples that fit into it. This organizer is particularly helpful for students who are learning the concept of categorization. The organizer emphasizes clusters of vocabulary words that are linked. The examples are usually concrete nouns that are the easiest and first words we learn in acquiring a language.

Procedures:

1. Choose the name of a category or class that has members which are familiar to you and your students.

2. Write the name in the base of the shell.

3. Brainstorm with the class a list of examples that fit into the chosen category.

4. Enter the name of one example inside each section of the shell.

5. Draw or write a description of each example above its name.

6. Discuss the characteristics that each of the examples share that define the category or class.

Variations:

⊙ Provide a See Shell containing several examples and descriptions and have the students name the category or class.

⊙ Introduce a number of objects belonging to several classes. Label a see shell template with each class name. Have a group of students sort the objects and enter their names and descriptions on the appropriate See Shell.

⊙ For ESL students, provide a see shell that has the name of the category/class and a picture of each example. Have them provide the label—in both English and their first language.

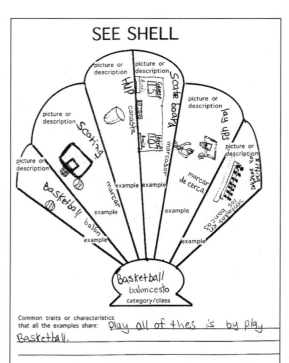

An ESL student created this map for his teacher, Luci Huizinga, who teaches for the Broome-Tioga Board of Cooperative Education Services in Newark Valley, New York. Sloan M. Johnson added the Spanish terms.

50 Graphic Organizers for Reading, Writing, and More
Scholastic Professional Books, 1999

Name_____ Date _____

See Shell

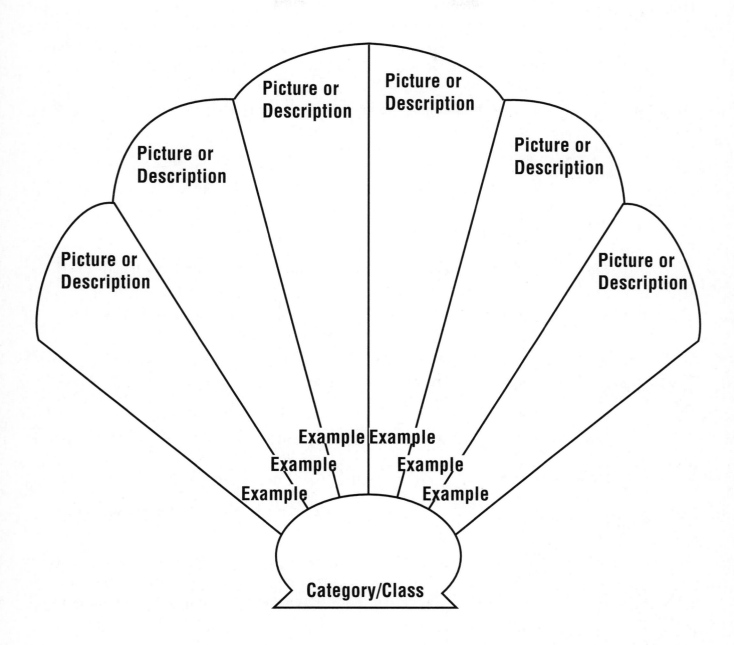

Common traits or characteristics that all the examples share:

_____

_____

_____

_____

T-Chart

Description: The T-chart focuses students' attention on the verbal and nonverbal attributes of a concept, process, or object. It helps students describe what something *looks like* and *sounds like*. Using these multiple senses helps students understand and remember.

Procedures:

1. Display the template on a chart or an overhead projector.

2. At the top of the template, write the concept, process, or object to be described.

3. Familiarize students with the T-chart by modeling its use.

4. Have students brainstorm what the concept, object, or process *looks like* and *sounds like*.

5. Write their responses under the appropriate column and then discuss.

Variations:

⊙ Use the T-chart to describe management issues, for example, appropriate cafeteria behavior, safe and effective fire drills, and so on.

⊙ Use the T-chart to describe processes used in the classroom, social skills such as cooperative learning, effective labs, peer revision, and so on.

⊙ Have the T-chart serve as a double-entry journal form.

⊙ Change column headings and use the T-chart as a prewriting strategy when writing a *compare* and *contrast* piece or *pro* and *con* piece.

⊙ Encourage younger students or ESL learners to draw pictures to represent ideas.

⊙ Change headings to FI (Facts In) and FO (Facts Out). Have students list what they already know about a topic under FI and their questions under FO and research the answers to FO questions.

⊙ As an assessment tool, list previously studied concepts, (generalizations, or principles) in the left-hand column. Have students write content-specific examples of each in the right-hand column.

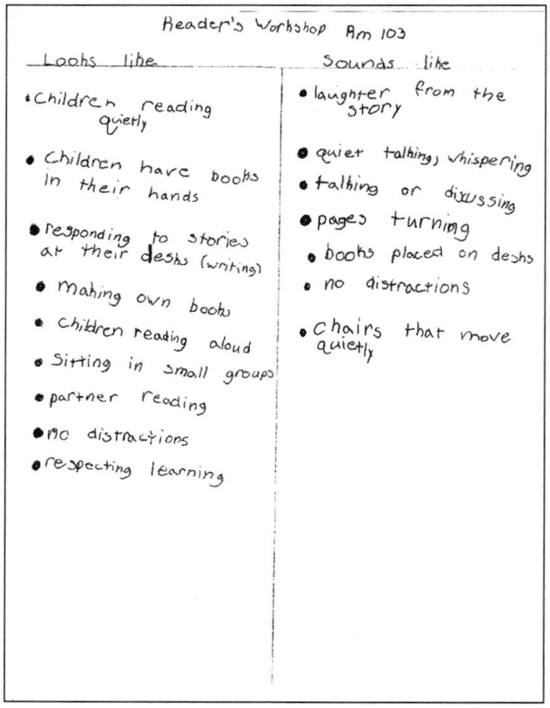

Angela Elsbree's class at Tioga Hills Elementary School in Vestal, New York, created this T-Chart on Readers' Workshop.

Reader's Workshop Rm 103

Looks like	Sounds like
• Children reading quietly	• laughter from the story
• Children have books in their hands	• quiet talking, whispering
• responding to stories at their desks (writing)	• talking or discussing
• making own books	• pages turning
• Children reading aloud	• books placed on desks
• Sitting in small groups	• no distractions
• partner reading	• Chairs that move quietly
• no distractions	
• respecting learning	

T-Chart

Three-Word Main Idea Map

Description: Use this organizer after reading, viewing, or listening to identify the main idea of a selection or presentation. It encourages broad interpretations of what constitutes the main idea but requires learners to support their ideas with specific information from the text or presentation.

Procedures:

1. Have students read, view, or listen to a selection or presentation.

2. Tell students to choose three main-idea words that seem important to them about the overall message of what they read, saw, or heard.

3. Have them put each main-idea word in one of the ovals on the map and then draw "spokes" radiating from each oval.

4. Students can find details from the selection or presentation that supports each main idea word and write them on or at the end of each spoke. (If they can't find details to support a word, choose a different main-idea word.)

5. In the box, have them write the main idea of the selection or presentation in a sentence using the three words they chose.

Variations:

⊙ Have ESL students or students with language difficulties draw a picture for each word they choose and an illustration for their sentence.

⊙ To build vocabulary knowledge, have students work in pairs and then in groups of four to share their main-idea words and why they chose them. Then make a list of all the main-idea words the class identifies and discuss each word and the personal meanings that emerge.

⊙ Encourage students to share their main idea sentences in small groups and/or as a class to build awareness of different interpretations.

⊙ Help students revise their main idea sentences by adding one or more supporting details, for example, add adjectives to nouns and adverbs to verbs.

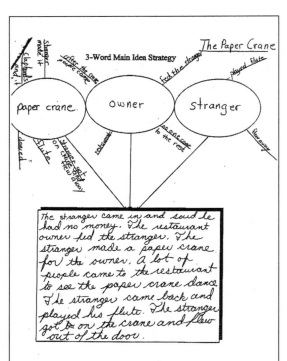

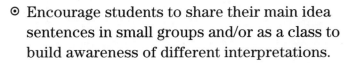

Diane Leskow's fourth grade class at T. J. Watson Elementary School in Endicott, New York, analyzed The Paper Crane *by looking at the crane, its owner, and the stranger.*

74

Three-Word Main Idea Map

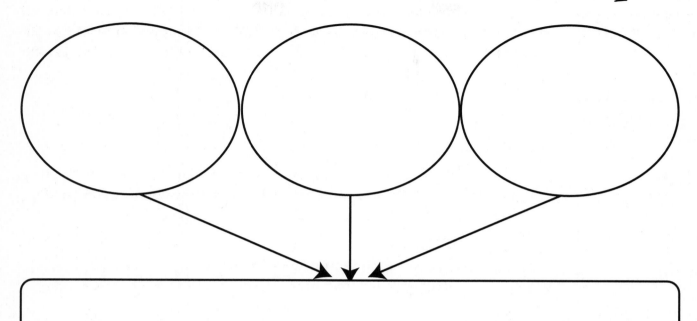

Vee Map

Description: The vee map developed by Novak and Gowin (1981) illustrates the process of scientific thinking and investigation. This organizer helps students focus on the various steps and the types of knowledge needed for research investigations.

Procedures:

1. Construct the vee and place the research topic at the top center.

2. Identify the key theories that form the basis of the investigation and write them at the top-left side of the vee.

3. Discuss and record the relevant principles and key concepts that are important in this investigation and put them in the appropriate spaces on the left side of the vee. You may wish to represent the concepts in a small graphic organizer.

4. At the bottom point of the vee, identify and write the research question.

5. Place the tools that can be used to research the question in the center of the vee.

6. As the research is conducted, record the information or data generated or collected at the bottom right. This can be done using words, symbols, or drawings.

7. Complete the right side of the vee by recording an analysis of the data, conclusions, and implications.

Variation:

⊙ Provide all of the information except conclusions and implications to provide an opportunity for students to practice using scientific investigations as the basis for judgments and decisions.

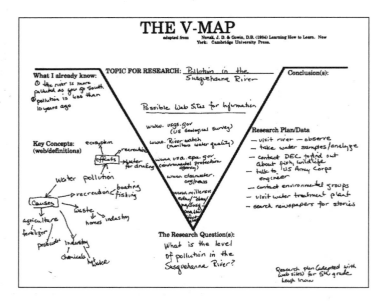

The information for this vee map was adapted by Leigh Irwin, who researched the Web sites that would be useful and included them in the center of the vee.

The Vee Map

TOPIC FOR RESEARCH: _____

Conclusion(s):

Research Tools:

Research Plan/Date:

What I already know:

Key Concepts: (web/definitions)

The Research Question(s):

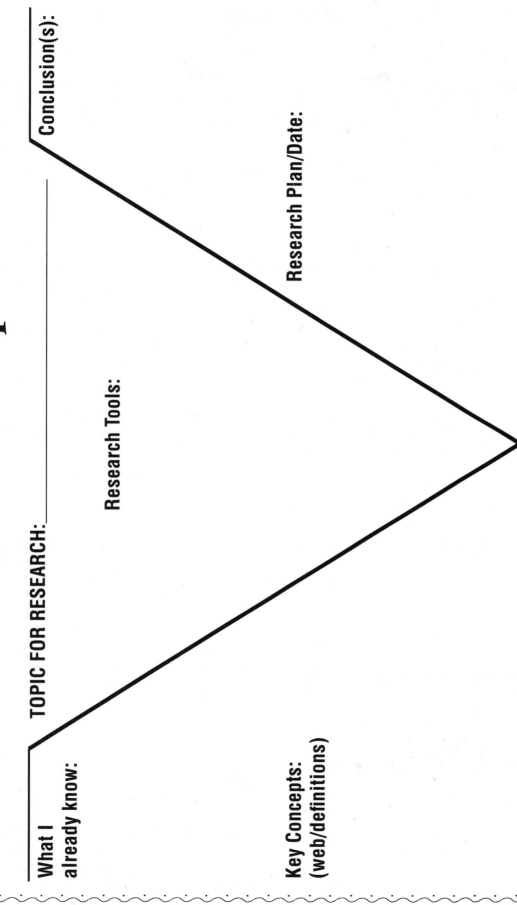

Adapted from Novak, J.D. and Gowin, D.B. (1984) *Learning How to Learn.* New York: Cambridge University Press.

Venn Diagram

Description: A Venn diagram consists of two (or sometimes as many as five) overlapping circles. It is used to represent information that is being compared and contrasted. The Venn diagram is one type of conceptual organizer that highlights similarities and differences.

Procedures:

1. Copy the Venn diagram template for students.

2. Identify and label above each circle the two people, places, or things to compare and contrast.

3. Discuss the similarities and differences with students.

4. Record shared traits or characteristics in the overlapping section of the circles.

5. Record unique traits and list them in the appropriate circle.

Variations:

⊙ Encourage students to reflect upon why they organized, sorted, and classified specific critical attributes. You might also have them think about the things they omitted.

⊙ Use three to five overlapping circles to compare three to five topics in any content subject. For example, students could compare five world cultures.

⊙ Implement this organizer as a postreading and viewing tool to assess students' comprehension.

⊙ Have students use the Venn diagram as a prewriting strategy when writing a comparative paper.

⊙ Form cooperative groups and have students share and compare the information listed on each Venn.

⊙ Encourage younger and ESL students to draw pictures to represent ideas.

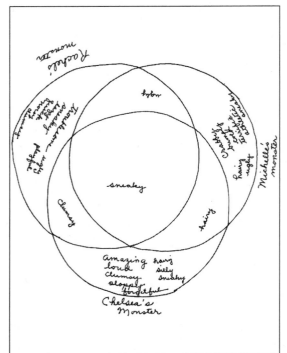

As part of a study on adjectives, Nancy B. Hargrave had her students invent their own monsters. She used a triple Venn to compare their creations. Nancy is a teacher at Glenwood Elementary School in Vestal, New York.

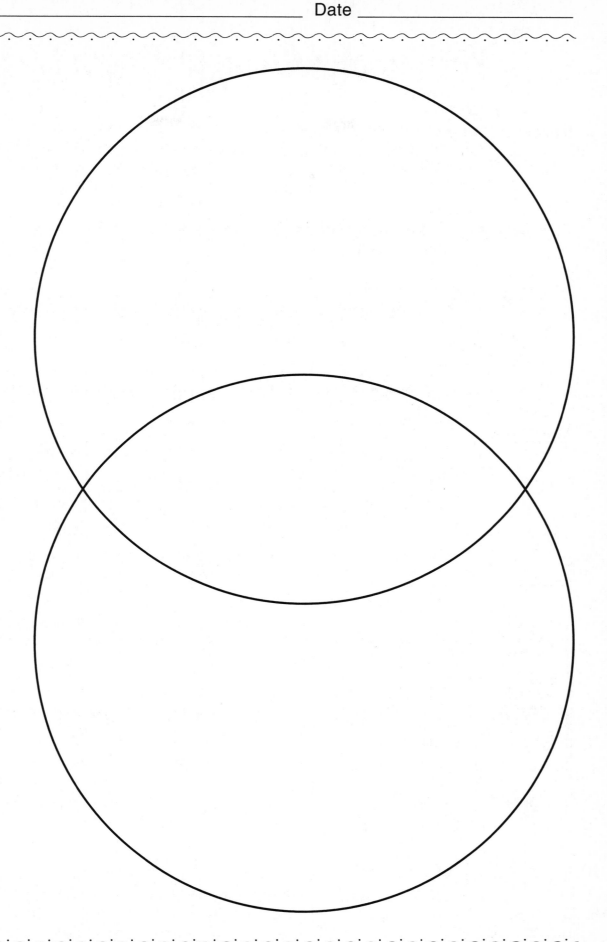

Venn Diagram

Vocabulary Concept Organizer

Description: This organizer displays visually the key components that were identified by Frayer as critical in the acquisition of new concepts (Frayer, Frederick, and Klausmeier, 1969). Often, students memorize definitions rather than engage in active negotiation of the meanings of various concepts. Frayer's model promotes a well-grounded understanding of the concept. While it is more time-consuming than traditional approaches, it promotes deeper understanding and longer retention.

Procedures:

1. Select a concept. Put it in the central square in the organizer.

2. In the upper left box, have students identify and record the essential characteristics or attributes of the concept.

3. In the upper right box, have students identify and record the characteristics that might be mistakenly associated with the concept.

4. In the bottom left box, give students several examples of the concept and discuss why they are examples. Then have students give their own examples of the concept.

5. In the bottom right box, provide several nonexamples of the concept and discuss why they are not examples. Then have students think of nonexamples and explain why they are nonexamples.

Variations:

- Identify four to six key concepts for a lesson or unit. Divide the class into groups, one group for each concept. Have each group complete an organizer for its concept and discuss it with the group.

- Provide an organizer that is complete except for the concept and have students guess the concept.

- Have students complete organizers of key concepts as a review procedure. Use completed organizers to assess students' understanding, clarify misconceptions, and reteach, if necessary.

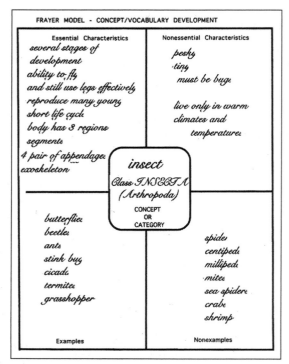

FRAYER MODEL - CONCEPT/VOCABULARY DEVELOPMENT

Essential Characteristics
several stages of development
ability to fly and still use legs effectively
reproduce many young
short life cycle
body has 3 regions segments
4 pair of appendages
exoskeleton

Nonessential Characteristics
pesky
tiny
must be bugs
live only in warm climates and temperatures

insect
Class INSECTA (Arthropoda)
CONCEPT OR CATEGORY

Examples
butterflies
beetles
ants
stink bug
cicada
termites
grasshopper

Nonexamples
spiders
centipede
millipede
mites
sea spiders
crabs
shrimp

Using information gathered from a Web-site search, this organizer clarifies the concept "insect."

Vocabulary Concept Development

ESSENTIAL CHARACTERISTICS

NONESSENTIAL CHARACTERISTICS

CONCEPT OR CATEGORY

EXAMPLES

NONEXAMPLES

Who Am I? Introductory Map

Description: This conceptual map shows icons that represent categories of information about a person. Students can use this map to introduce themselves to one another at the beginning of the year or when they first form small groups to get to know each other better.

Procedures:

1. Have each student write his or her name in the center of the template.

2. For each icon that represents a category of information, have students draw pictures and/or label each with words to show supporting information.

Variations:

⊙ Add to or change this template by including different icons.

⊙ Have students use this template to write an autobiography.

⊙ Have students put their maps on overhead transparencies and share them.

⊙ Students can use this map to explore a character in a story, a historical figure, or a real person they are studying.

⊙ Read or have students read randomly chosen "Who Am I?" maps so the class can guess who the map is about.

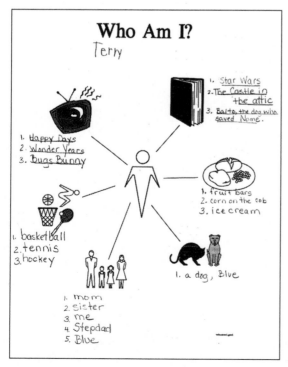

Terry Brewer of Endicott, New York, created this map for her mother, Sheri.

Who Am I?

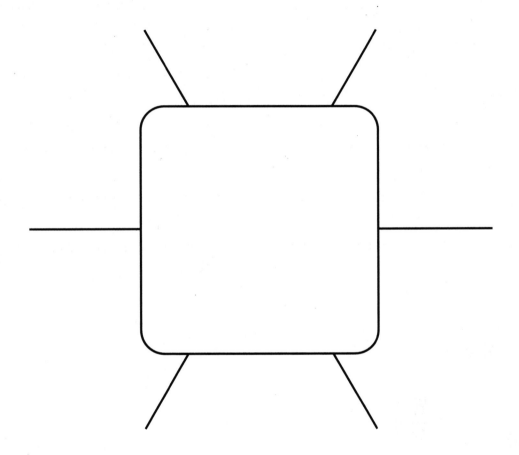

Word Tree

Description: A word tree contains the words that originate from a root or base word. Word trees show learners how related words "grow" from a common root or base (for example, Greek, Latin, and so on) and possess similar meanings because of their shared foundation. Creating word trees requires knowledge of structural analysis and syllabication skills, and encourages dictionary use.

Procedures:

1. Begin by asking students to identify the root word that is the common element in three or four words, for example, *graph*.

2. Write the root word on the template at the base of the tree trunk.

3. Use a dictionary to find the meaning of the root.

4. Ask students for other examples of words that share the common root and discuss the similarities of their meanings.

5. Write each example on a separate branch of the tree.

6. Use the dictionary to determine word meanings and find other words containing the same root.

Variations:

⊙ Write word meanings on the tree as a vocabulary activity.

⊙ Use this strategy in science or social studies with technical vocabulary from a unit of study.

⊙ Form cooperative groups and make dictionaries available for each group. Have each group create a word tree for a different root or base. Have groups share their word trees with each member responsible for explaining some of the words the group created.

⊙ Randomly assign root or base words to individual students or pairs who can then create their own word trees for display on a bulletin board, for example, "Greek and Latin Roots," or inclusion in a class dictionary.

⊙ Use a list of common prefixes and suffixes to help students create words from the root and write each on one of the tree's branches.

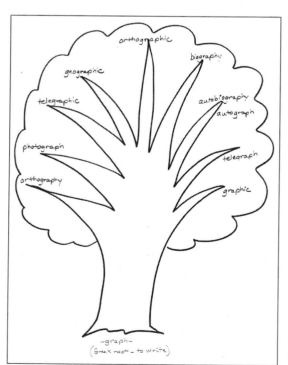

This word tree was created to help students see some of the words derived from the root graph.

Name_____ Date _____

Word Tree

Root Word

Book Summary Organizer

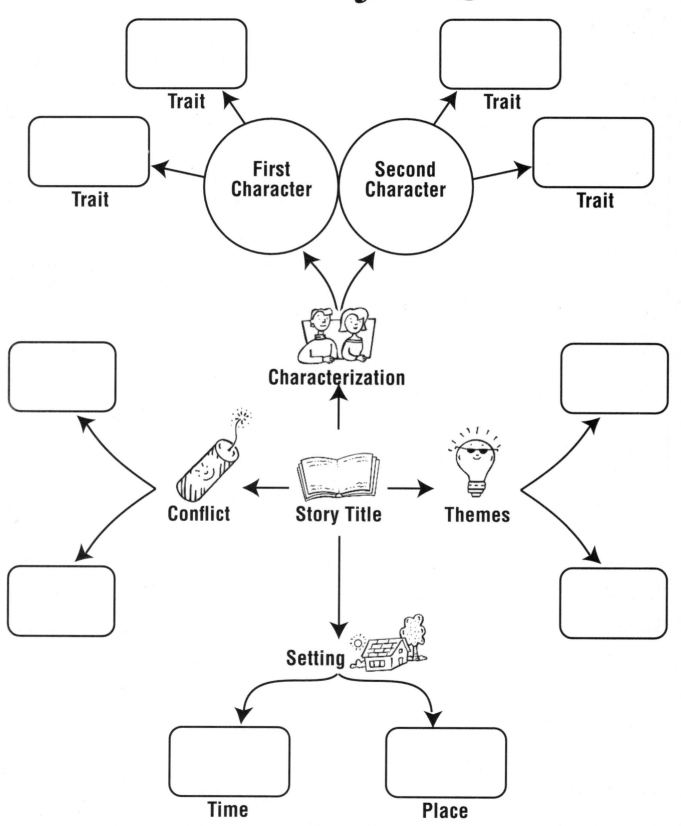

Trait

Trait

First Character

Second Character

Trait

Trait

Characterization

Conflict

Story Title

Themes

Setting

Time

Place

50 GRAPHIC ORGANIZERS FOR READING, WRITING, AND MORE
Scholastic Professional Books, 1999

Name____________________ Date ____________

Decision-Making Guide

THE QUESTION: ______________________________

____

Option 1	Option 2	Option 3

Pros	Cons	Pros	Cons	Pros	Cons

Option chosen: ______________________________

Reasons: ______________________________

____

____

Predicted/possible outcomes: ______________________________

____

____

____

K-W-L Sequence Chart

TOPIC:_____

What I already know:

What I want to learn:

What I learned:

How I will go about learning:

Where I might look for more information:

What I still want to know:

50 GRAPHIC ORGANIZERS FOR READING, WRITING, AND MORE
Scholastic Professional Books, 1999

Planning Organizer

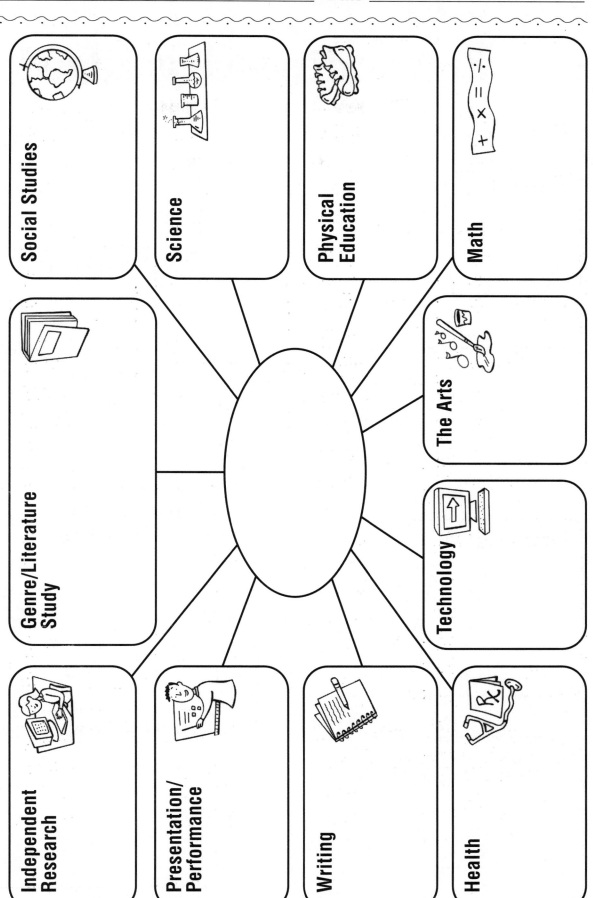

Social Studies

Science

Physical Education

Math

Genre/Literature Study

The Arts

Technology

Independent Research

Presentation/ Performance

Writing

Health

Name_____   Date _____

Prereading Organizer

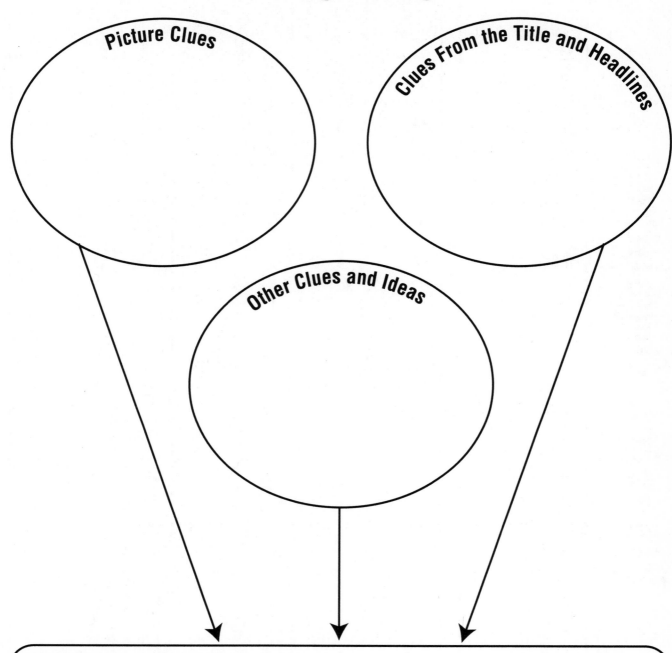

Picture Clues

Clues From the Title and Headlines

Other Clues and Ideas

My Predictions About the Reading

50 GRAPHIC ORGANIZERS FOR READING, WRITING, AND MORE
Scholastic Professional Books, 1999

Name_____ Date _____

Reading and Writing
Goal Pyramid

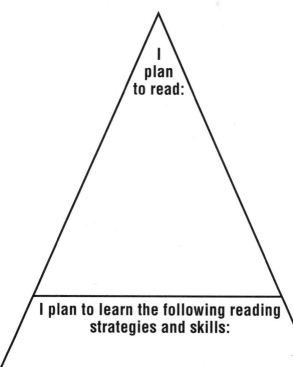

I
plan
to read:

I plan to learn the following reading
strategies and skills:

I plan to write:

I plan to learn the following writing strategies and skills:

Self-Assessment Organizer

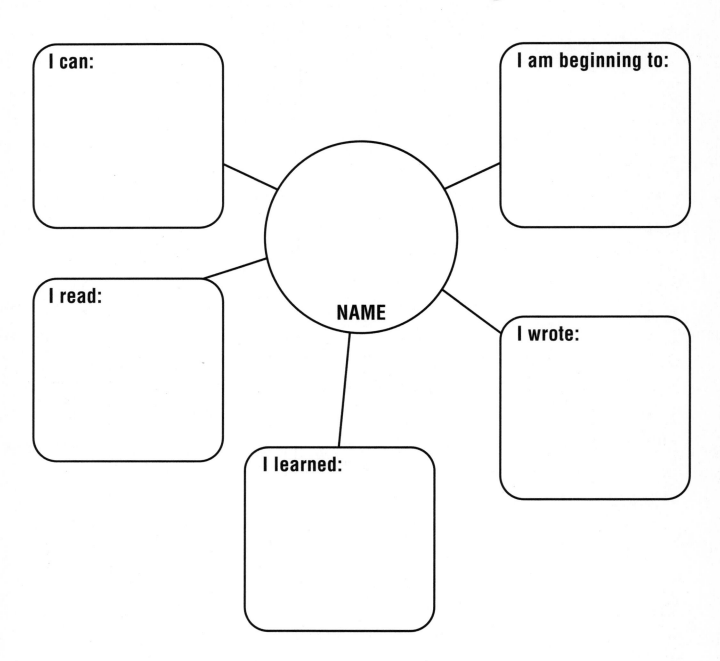

I can:

I am beginning to:

NAME

I read:

I wrote:

I learned:

My goals for next time are:

_____

_____

_____

_____

50 GRAPHIC ORGANIZERS FOR READING, WRITING, AND MORE
Scholastic Professional Books, 1999

Story Feeling/Event Timeline

TITLE: _____

AUTHOR: _____

ILLUSTRATOR: _____

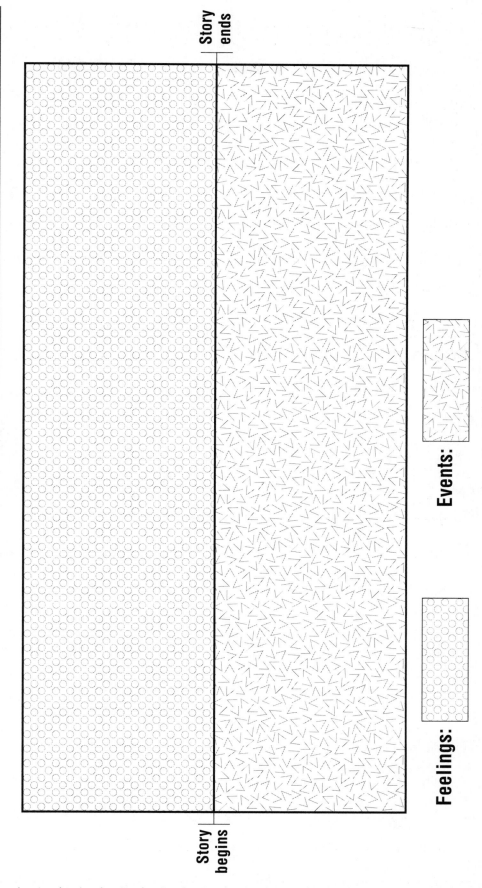

Story ends

Story begins

Events:

Feelings:

Timeline

TOPIC: _____

Pick out the important events in this history (or story). Put the first date on the line that reads "beginning" date and then put the event that happened on the slanted line above the date.

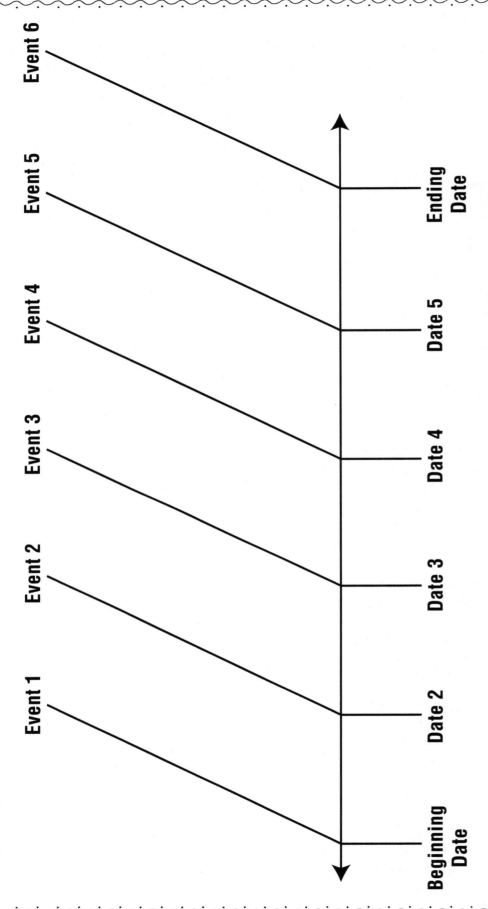

Event 1

Event 2

Event 3

Event 4

Event 5

Event 6

Beginning Date

Date 2

Date 3

Date 4

Date 5

Ending Date

50 GRAPHIC ORGANIZERS FOR READING, WRITING, AND MORE
Scholastic Professional Books, 1999

Using Many Sources

TOPIC: _____

People	
Books	
Magazines	
Newspapers	
Computer Searches	

REFERENCES

Alvermann, D.E. (1991). "The discussion web: A graphic aid for learning across the curriculum." *The Reading Teacher*, (45)2, 92–99.

Buzan, T. (1995) *The Mind Map Book, 2nd ed.* London, UK: BBC

Checkley, Kathy (1997). "The first seven...and the eighth: A conversation with Howard Gardner." *Educational Leadership, 55* (1), 8–13.

Dulthie, J. (1986). "The Web: A powerful tool for the teaching and evaluation of the expository essay." *The History and Social Science Teacher*, 21, 232–236.

Frayer, D. A., Frederick, W. D., and Klausmeier, H. J. (1969). *A schema for testing the level of concept mastery* (Working Paper No. 16). Madison, WI: Wisconsin Research and Development Center for Cognitive Learning.

Gardner, Howard (1993). *Multiple Intelligences.* New York: Basic Books.

Gardner, Howard (1997). "Multiple intelligences as a partner in school improvement." *Educational Leadership*, SS(1), 20–21.

Kagan, S. (1994). *Cooperative Learning.* San Clemente, CA.: Resources for Teachers.

Readance, J.E., Bean, T.W., and Baldwin, R.S.(1998). *Content Area Literacy (6th ed.).* Dubuque, IA: Kendall Hunt.

Schwartz, R. and Raphael, T. (1985). "Concept of definition: A key to improving students' vocabulary." *The Reading Teacher*, (39), 676–682.

PART III

Writing Organizer Templates, Strategies, and Student Samples

Assessment Y-Pie Map

Description: The Y-Pie focuses on self-assessment of a written draft. Using three questions, it moves the students from strengths to strategies for revision.

Procedures:

1. Introduce students to the Y-Pie Map by modeling its use with one of your own compositions.

2. Have students reread their piece focusing on the three questions stated in the Y-Pie.

3. Use different colored pens or symbols to mark things students like and things to change.

4. Fill in sections 1 and 2 with specific characteristics and/ or quotes from the piece.

5. Brainstorm strategies and specific options to improve the piece and record in section 3.

Variations:

⊙ Generate ideas for the Y-Pie Map in a peer conference or a teacher-student conference.

⊙ Use the Y-Pie to evaluate media presentations or projects.

⊙ By changing the questions in the Y, this can be used for a variety of products:

-What is the question or problem?

-What data do I have?

-What procedure(s) do I use to solve the problem?

⊙ Place the Y-Pie with the rough draft in students' writing folders to document the writing process.

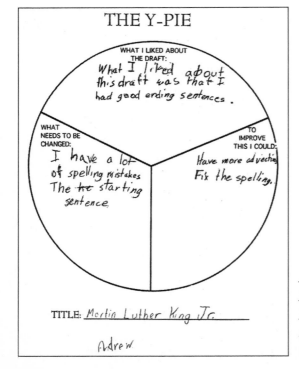

THE Y-PIE

WHAT I LIKED ABOUT THE DRAFT:
What I liked about this draft was that I had good ending sentences.

WHAT NEEDS TO BE CHANGED:
I have a lot of spelling mistakes. The starting sentence.

TO IMPROVE THIS I COULD:
Have more adveching Fix the spelling.

TITLE: _Martin Luther King Jr._

Andrew

Andrew Riley, a fourth grader at Perry Brown School in Norwich, New York, assessed his writing piece on Martin Luther King, Jr., in this organizer. The students suggested to their teacher, Linda Hoffman, that she use the Y-Pie Map to give them feedback on their writing.

Name_____ Date _____

Y-Pie

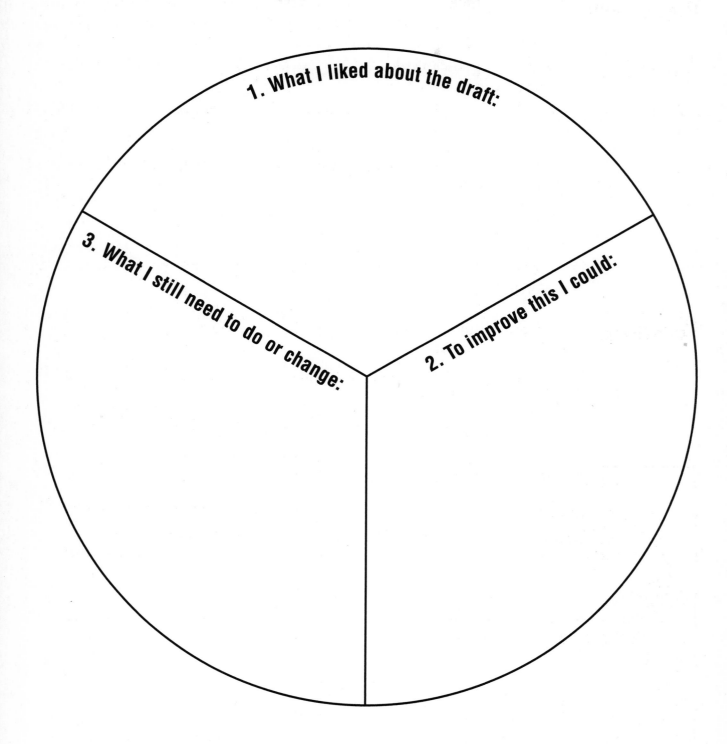

Feedback sheet for self- or peer-evaluation of writing.

Central Idea Organizer

Description: Writing about a central idea is a common task for students. This organizer shows students some of the types of information they might want to include in their compositions. It also provides some key connecting words to help them express and link ideas.

Procedures:

1. Have each student decide upon the main idea for his or her composition and record the idea in the MAIN IDEA box on the template. To help students vary their language, encourage students to think of some other words to use for the main idea and also list them in the box.

2. Instruct students to supply information to fill in each of the six boxes on the template.

3. Let students think about the ideas listed and ask for other ideas that are important to include in the composition. Add them to the organizer by creating new boxes.

4. Ask if there are any ideas that are not important and have students cross out those boxes.

5. Have students decide which information should come first, second, etc., in their compositions and number the boxes in this order.

6. Encourage students to look at the words in small print at the bottom of each box. These words help writers express ideas and connect one idea or sentence with another as they draft their compositions.

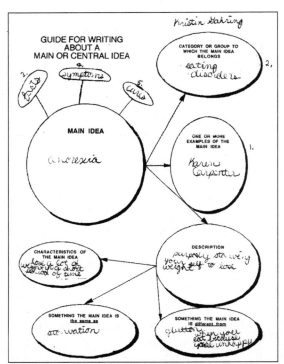

Variations:

⊙ Use the organizer to take notes about main ideas and concepts from a chapter or section of a science or social studies text.

⊙ Use the organizer to review an important topic for a test.

⊙ Brainstorm images for a poem based on a central idea by using the template.

Kristin Gahring, an eighth grader in Lizanne McTigue's class at Vestal Middle School in Vestal, New York, completed this organizer to guide her composition about anorexia.

Name_____ Date _____

Guide For Writing About a Main or Central Idea

Category or Group to Which the Main Idea Belongs

Is an example of...one type of...is included in...belongs to

Main Idea

Synonyms or other words to express the main idea

One or More Examples of the Main Idea

For instance...for example... an example...such as

Description

Looks like....sounds like...feels like...smells like...tastes like... appears...seems...

Characteristics of the Main Idea

These traits. . . characteristics

Something the Main Idea is *the same as*

Resembles...is like...is similar to... is the same as...reminds me of...

Something the Main Idea´is *different from*

Contrasts with...is the opposite of... is not like...differs from

Comparison Organizer

Description: This organizer is a guide for writing a comparison/contrast composition. It also provides some key organizing words (connectives) to help structure the paper.

Procedures:

1. Have students decide on two (or more) items to compare and write them in the ovals on each side of the organizer.

2. Encourage students to think about the ways the two items are the same. Then have student(s) record the similarities in the box labeled SAME.

3. Let students think about the ways the items are different and record the differences in the box labeled DIFFERENT.

4. Instruct students to decide the order in which to tell about the likenesses and the differences between the items and number them.

5. Examine with student(s) the words that can be used to talk about items that are the same and items that are different. Tell students to choose and circle the key words on the template that will help organize the writing.

6. Have students use the organizer as a guide for writing the comparison.

7. Remind students to check the template to see that all of the ideas on the organizer are in the comparison paper.

Variations:

⊙ Use the organizer to compare two books.

⊙ Use the organizer to compare the same item, place, or person at two different times.

⊙ Use the organizer to compare predictions with what really happened.

⊙ Assign students one item and let them choose the other item to compare.

⊙ Have students identify the key organizing words in a book or a section of text and talk about how they help the reader understand the information.

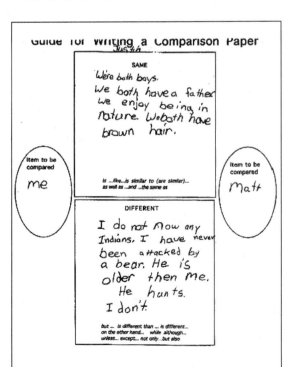

Rose Rotzler had her middle school students compare themselves with Matt or Attean, characters in The Sign of the Beaver.

50 GRAPHIC ORGANIZERS FOR READING, WRITING, AND MORE
Scholastic Professional Books, 1999

Guide for Writing a Comparison Paper

SAME

Is like…is similar to (are similar)…as well as…and…the same as

Item to be compared

Item to be compared

DIFFERENT

But…is different from…is different…on the other hand…while although… unless…except…not only…but also

Persuade 4B Map

Description: This map serves as a blueprint to support persuasive writing. It requires students to identify not only the best evidence in support of an argument, but also an acknowledgment of opposing opinions.

Procedures:

1. Tell students to read a selection/s on a debatable topic.

2. Lead a class discussion of ideas and facts to support both sides of the debate.

3. Have students choose a position on one side or the other.

4. Help students identify who they will persuade. Explain that an audience is often best persuaded with the strongest evidence and arguments presented first, and at least one opposing opinion noted.

5. Tell students to use words such as *should, ought,* or *must* to write a position statement in the INTRODUCTION box on the template.

6. Next, have students write the three best reasons to support their position in the BEST EVIDENCE spaces, and one example of opposing evidence in the BUT space.

7. Then have students restate or paraphrase their position and write it in the CONCLUSION box on the template.

8. Have students reread, add, delete, and edit each sentence in their paragraphs before rewriting and sharing it.

4 B Map for Persuasive Writing
Drawing by Tobby

Introduction (Position or Purpose):
You should try drawing. It is really fun to do when your bord.

Best: Drawing is fun cause soon as you get drawing you can draw.

Best: I start it drawing when I was 4 and I did funny things.

Best: Sometimes when I'm drawing I can't find nothing to draw, So I pictured it in my mind and I got it.

But: So when you draw think in your imaginson!

Conclusion (Restate or Paraphrase Position):
Drawing is easy when you get it. So when you draw don't copy it just use your imangson.

Variations:

⊙ Have students reread and renumber their BEST reasons, or add words such as *first, second, third,* and *last.*

⊙ Conduct peer conferences for revision before students rewrite what they create independently.

⊙ Use this map after your students complete a discussion web.

⊙ Pair struggling students with stronger students to do this map after you model or explain it.

Sha-Tobbya Thomas, a student in Diane Leskow's fourth-grade class at T. J. Watson Elementary School in Crestview Heights, New York, created this organizer to convince others to try drawing.

50 GRAPHIC ORGANIZERS FOR READING, WRITING, AND MORE
Scholastic Professional Books, 1999

4B Map for Persuasive Writing

**Introduction
(Position or Purpose):**

**BEST
(Evidence):**

**BEST
(Evidence):**

**BEST
(Evidence):**

**BUT
(Opposing Evidence):**

**Conclusion
(Restate or Paraphrase Position):**

Problem-Solution Organizer

Description: The critical thinking necessary to problem-solve by posing and evaluating solutions is an important skill students need throughout their lives. Being able to write clearly and persuasively about proposed solutions is as important as being able to think clearly and logically in formulating solutions. This writing guide helps students organize and write about problems and proposed solutions.

Procedures:

1. Have students identify a problem and write it in the diamond at the top of the template labeled PROBLEM.

2. Ask student(s) to think about what specifically makes this a problem. Have the students write the specific evidence for defining this as a problem in the box labeled EVIDENCE. (See note below.)

3. Let students list each of the possible solutions in the appropriate box and circle the ones they think are the best.

4. Have students predict and write the results expected from the chosen solutions in the box labeled RESULTS.

5. Students then write a persuasive paper arguing that the circled solutions should be implemented, using the template as a guide. Remind students to use the key organizing words to help connect ideas.

Variations:

⊙ Instead of choosing a solution and arguing for it, use the template to define and describe a problem, its possible solutions, and the pros and cons of each possible solution.

⊙ Use the template to guide a class or group brainstorming session on class conflicts or school behavior problems.

⊙ Use the template as a guide for making a multimedia presentation about a school or community problem.

⊙ Suggest that students work in pairs or small groups to complete the template on the same topic and compare the results.

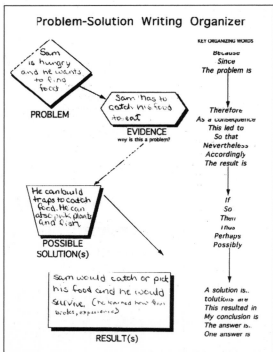

Lynda DeLuca and Lynne Eckert worked with sixth-grade students at Ann G. McGuinness School in Endicott, New York, to generate writing organizers based on Sam's problem in My Side of the Mountain.

106

Problem-Solution Organizer

PROBLEM

EVIDENCE
Why is this a problem?

POSSIBLE SOLUTION(S)

RESULT(S)

Key Organizing Words

Because
Since
The problem is

↓

Therefore
As a consequence
This led to
So that
Nevertheless
Accordingly
The result is

↓

If
So
Then
Thus
Perhaps
Possibly

↓

A solution is
Solutions are
This resulted in
My conclusion is
The answer is
One answer is

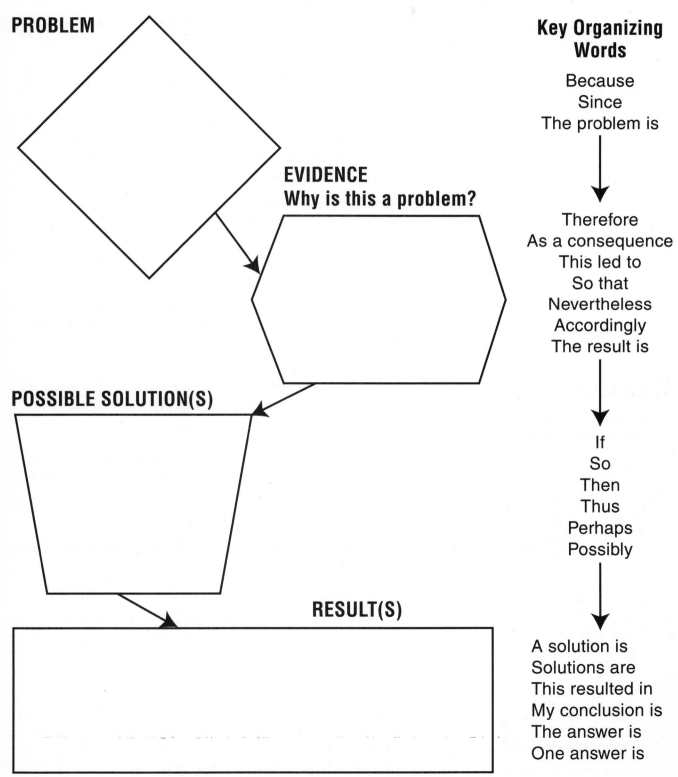

What Happened Organizer

Description: This organizer helps students understand chronological organization. It provides a plan for writing and some of the key organizing words or connectives to put ideas together in a sequence. Chronological organization is central to most narratives, much historical writing, recipes, procedures, and directions.

Procedures:

1. Have students decide on their topic. Be sure it is appropriate for a time-order or chronological pattern. Have them write in the title.

2. Instruct students to write the first event in BOX 1; the second in BOX 2; the third in BOX 3; and the final event, the conclusion, in BOX 4.

3. Point out the organizing words at the left side of each box. Have students choose from the key organizing words to start sentences and connect ideas. You may want to have students circle the words they use in each box.

4. Encourage students to use this organizer as an outline for their paper.

Variations:

⊙ Choose the topic and key organizing words rather than having students choose. The class can then write a group story. This is an excellent way to introduce the use of this organizer and to help students understand chronological order.

⊙ Have students who speak other languages identify the key organizing words or connectives in their languages. This can be used in foreign language classes or as a way to help ESL students understand how to use English connectives.

⊙ Let students identify the key organizing words in a picture book, a historical selection, a newspaper account, a recipe, or any other chronological account. Add them to the template.

⊙ Brainstorm other key organizing words that could be used in a narrative and add them to the template.

⊙ Encourage students to think about how we understand the time-order sequence in movies, television, and plays without key connecting words.

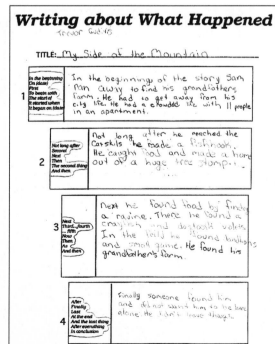

Lynne Eckert and Lynda DeLuca used this organizer to organize what happened in the novel My Side of the Mountain. *Then they had their sixth graders at Ann G. McGuinness School, Endicott, New York, use the template to plan for writing their own adventure stories.*

Name_____ Date _____

Writing About What Happened

TITLE:_____

1

In the beginning
On (date)
First
To begin with
The start of
It started when
It began on (date)

2

Not long after
Second
Next
Then
The second thing
And then

3

Next
Third…fourth…fifth
Now
Then
As
And then

4

After
Finally
Last
At the end
And the last thing
After everything
In conclusion

50 GRAPHIC ORGANIZERS FOR READING, WRITING, AND MORE
Scholastic Professional Books, 1999

Appendices

Appendix A

Print Resources

Bellanca, J. A. (1992). *The Cooperative Think Tank II: Graphic Organizers to Teach Thinking in the Cooperative Classroom.* Palatine, IL: Skylight Press.

Bromley, K., Irwin-DeVitis, L., and Modlo, M. (1995*). Graphic Organizers: Visual Strategies for Active learning.* New York: Scholastic Professional Books.

Bromley, K. D. (1995). *Webbing With Literature: Creating Story Maps With Children's Books*, 2nd ed. Boston: Allyn & Bacon.

Cassidy, J. (1992). "Help your students get the main idea with graphic organizers." *Learning, 21* (2), 75–77.

Cassidy, J. (1991). "Using graphic organizers to develop critical thinking." *Gifted Child Quarterly, 12* (6), 34–36.

Clarke, John. *Patterns of thinking.* Burlington, VT: Department of Education, University of Vermont.

Hanselman, C.A. (1990). "Using brainstorming webs in the mathematics classroom." *Mathematics Teaching in the Middle School, 1* (9), 766–70.

Heimlich, J. E. and Pittleman, S. D. (1986). *Semantic mapping: Classroom applications.* Newark, DE: International Reading Association.

Hyerle, D. (1996). "Thinking maps: Seeing is understanding." *Educational Leadership, 53* (4), 85–89.

Irwin-DeVitis, L. and Pease, D. (1995). "Using graphic organizers for learning and assessment in middle level classrooms." *Middle School Journal, 26*(5), 57–64.

Lehman, H. (1992). *Graphic organizers benefit slow learners.* Clearinghouse, *66*(1), 53–55.

Novak, J. (1981). *Learning How to Learn.* New York: Cambridge University Press.

Parks, S. and Black, H. (1990). *Organizing Thinking*, Book 1. Pacific Grove, CA: Critical Thinking Press and Software.

Parks, S. and Black, H. (1992). *Organizing Thinking*, Book 2. Pacific Grove, CA: Critical Thinking Press and Software.

Sinatra, R., et al. (1994). "Using a computer-based semantic mapping, reading, and writing approach with at-risk fourth graders." *Journal of Computing in Childhood Education, 5* (1), 93–112.

Appendix B

Web Sites for Graphic Organizers

http://www.graphic org
How graphic organizers can help you and your students

http://home.earthlink.net/~tsdobbs/go.htm
Examples and instructions on using graphic organizers

http://www.fromnowon.org/oct97/picture.html
Graphic organizers as thinking tools

http://www.indiana.edu/~eric_rec/ieo/bibs/graphele.html
Graphic organizers in elementary schools - bibliography - ERIC
Clearinghouse

http://www.inspiration.com
Organizers created using Inspiration® software

http://w3.ag.uiuc.edu/AIM/Discovery/Mind/c-m2.html
Kinds of concept maps

http://www.sdcoe.k12.ca.us/score/actbank/torganiz.htm
Teacher directions for a variety of graphic organizers

http://www.gold.net:80/users/dx61/mapa.htm
The use of mind mapping (Tony Buzan)

http://www.history.org/other/teaching/tchmhvoc.htm
Vocabulary matrix used in history